# PROPHECIES AND PREDICTIONS

## FOR THE

# MILLENNIUM

# PROPHECIES AND PREDICTIONS
## FOR THE
# MILLENNIUM

PAUL ROLAND

ISLAND BOOKS

This edition published in 1997 by
Island Books
an imprint of S. Webb & Son (Distributors) Ltd.
Telford Place, Pentraeth Road
Menai Bridge
Isle of Anglesey LL59 5RW

This book created by Amazon Publishing Ltd.
Editors: Tessa Rose, Ray Granger
Design: wilson design associates
Repro: Master Image, Singapore
Printed in Italy

**Picture Credits**
The Publisher wishes to thank the following organisations for
permission to use their pictures in this book. Every effort has
been made to trace owners of pictures but should any picture
have been used without proper acknowledgement the
Publishers apologise.

AKG Photo London; Bridgeman Art Library: Peter Willi / National
Gallery, London / Giraudon; Corbis-Bettman; Edgar, *The Great
Pyramid: Its Time Features*, 1924; E. T Archive; Fortean Picture
Library; Hulton Deutsch Collection; Hulton Getty Picture Collection;
Kevin Redpath Photography; Library of Congress; Mary Evans Picture
Library; NASA; Peter Newark's Historical Pictures; Peter Newark's
Military Pictures; Popperfoto; Portfolio Pictures; Reuter; Rex
Features; Sathya Sai Book Centre; Science Photo Library; Sipa Press;
Taylor Photo Library; The Art dept., Transworld Publishers; The Harry
Price Collection; University of London; The Ronald Grant Archive.

# CONTENTS

# INTRODUCTION

People have always shared both a fascination with, and a fear of, the future. No matter what creed or culture we belong to, no matter how secure we might feel as individuals, we all share an innate curiosity about our future and the future of our planet. As we approach the new millennium this interest naturally intensifies – just as a new year offers the opportunity for reflection and a new beginning, so a new millennium promises much more. The pace of life has accelerated dramatically in the last hundred years, heightening our sense of urgency to live life to the full, to cram in all the richness and variety of experience the modern world has to offer. The approach of a new century and, more significantly, a new millennium, telescopes these hopes and fears to leave us with an acute awareness of own mortality.

But what will the next millennium bring? Will the year 2000 mark the dawn of a New Age for mankind, the Age of Aquarius and the coming of the Messiah, or will it herald Armageddon, the appearance of the Antichrist and the destruction envisaged by the apocalyptic prophets of the Old Testament and their modern disciples?

It's easy to dismiss the dire warnings of Divine retribution, but who can afford to ignore the recent climatic changes

which suggest that after decades of ecological exploitation nature may strike back, bringing decades of drought, famine, floods, earthquakes and plagues. Our fears for the future are highlighted by our increasing awareness of the fragility of the earth, of the threat to our survival posed by the destruction of the ozone layer, global warming, and even the possibility of a new Ice Age. There are, too, very real threats of our own making which we will face well into the next century — AIDS, economic recession, bacterial and perhaps even nuclear terrorism, critical overpopulation and pernicious global pollution. In the last two thousand years we have failed to master the forces of either Mother Nature or human nature.

Most of us imagine the future in terms of scientific progress, of ever greater technological advances and increased personal comfort, but it doesn't take a prophet to predict that human nature is unlikely to change significantly in the coming Millenium. In the future, as in the past, we are likely to remain the source of our own misery as well as of our salvation. Our capacity for self-destruction appears to run in parallel to our progress. The last thousand years have witnessed our ascent from the ignorance of the Dark Ages to our first tentative steps in space. Perhaps sometime in the next thousand years our descendants will receive an official visitation from another world in response, or maybe they will suffer the fallout from our scientific progress in the form of a nuclear holocaust to outrival the horrors foreseen by the Biblical visionaries.

Most of us can only guess as to which side of our nature will triumph, but there have been remarkable men and women throughout history who have claimed to have actually 'seen' the world as it will be in the future. Some of these individuals have been exposed as hysterical cranks, or as charlatans intent on exploiting the fears of the gullible and in a minority of cases of bringing about their own personal apocalypse. However, there are others whose pronouncements cannot be so readily dismissed.

Of course, personal visions are impossible to validate and it could also be argued that the symbolic nature of many predictions defies the efforts of both believers and detractors to interpret them. But whether we regard the psychics and seers as genuine or otherwise, the questions remain. Is it possible to foresee that which has not yet come to pass? And if it is, is it possible to alter it? Why do so many of us feel the need to believe in prophecy and why do a disturbing number of people blindly follow a false messiah, even to the point of bringing about their own destruction?

This book attempts to answer these questions by examining the prophecies and predictions made by psychics and seers throughout the ages for the year 2000 and beyond. Who were they, what exactly were their predictions and is there any basis for believ-

ing that some of them might come true? Is the future of mankind predetermined, as the predictions seem to indicate? And if the psychics and the seers truly have the ability to see far into the future, does that mean that we are all just puppets of Fate waiting in the wings to play out our parts at the whim of an omnipotent deity? Or, are we the masters of our own lives with the free will to influence the future, to contribute to the evolution of mankind, and perhaps even to bring about our own extinction?

# THE MEANING OF THE MILLENNIUM

The word 'millennium' is derived from the Latin *mille*, meaning 'a thousand', and *annus* meaning 'year'. For the Judaeo-Christian religions it has a deep, symbolic significance. It derives from the belief that the world had a clearly defined beginning and is heading inexorably towards a predetermined end.

For Christians the belief in the millennium derives from the Book of Revelation which predicts a thousand years of peace on earth following Christ's return to the world. It promises that the Messiah's appearance will be followed by the resurrection of the dead, the Last Judgement and universal salvation for all those judged to be just souls. The significance of the year 2000 derives from the belief that these events will take place 2000 years after Christ's birth, but this is confounded by the fact that the exact date of Christ's birth is unknown. The general consensus is that he was born in 4 BC, but that backdates the true beginning of the millennium to 1996!

However, there is a dissenting sect of Millenarianists who believe that the millennium refers instead to the thousand-year period prior to the Second Coming. While yet another group believes that the millennium is not a fixed event scheduled to arrive at a preordained date, but rather the idea of a new age of spiritual enlightenment which cannot be inaugurated until the dogmas and doctrines of orthodox religion are dispensed with, once and for all.

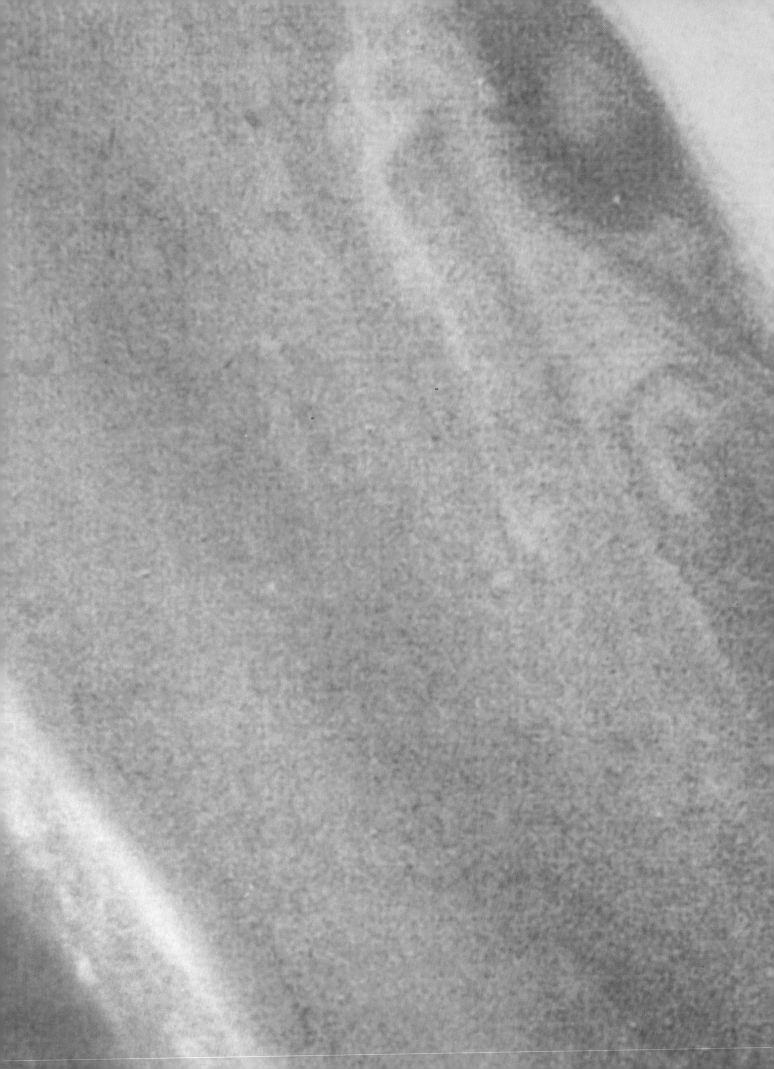

# APOCALYPSE NOW

For ancient civilizations time was cyclical like the seasons. It was a belief embodied in their mythologies. Each morning with the rising sun the gods would be seen to be bestowing their blessing on the people, and with the coming of night the holy men would appease the appropriate deity with ritual worship and sacrifice, so that life could continue as it always had done, without fear of the future.

It was only with the advent of monotheism, the belief in one omnipotent, omnipresent God, that the concept of creation with a definite beginning and a predetermined, finite end took hold on the popular imagination. To accommodate this belief, the concept of time had to be redefined as a linear progression. This led to a fascination with prophecy, precognition and prediction - the possibility of being able to look ahead to what destiny, or fate, has in store for us.

However, in attempting to impose order upon what they considered to be chaos, the founding fathers of orthodox religion denied the possibility of a greater reality which had been revealed to the prophets and mystics through visions. Only now, as we approach a new millennium, are such revelations beginning, once again, to be seen as the true purpose of prophecy.

# KALI YUGA – THE DARK AGE

**According to the Hindu and Buddhist traditions the Universe evolves through great cosmic cycles which follow the same pattern as the seasons and life itself. At the end of each complete cycle, or Manvantara, all life moves into a new stage of evolution. We are currently living in the final phase of the fourth Manvantara – the Dark Age – which will see catastrophic upheaval.**

The Manvantara is comprised of four distinct phases, or ages: Krita-yuga, Tetra-yuga, Dvapara-yuga and Kali-yuga. Presiding over our present age, the Kali-yuga, is the Hindu goddess Kali, the Goddess of Darkness, whom the Hindu scriptures prophesy will reign over a period of increasing materialism, progressive moral degeneration and pain, which are the birth pangs of a new human being for the new age to come. During this period the earth will also be subjected to violent change, to catastrophic climactic upheaval and disturbance of natural phenomena, during which the ice caps will melt and the people of all lands will suffer the consequences of severe drought and famine.

But the Hindu and Buddhist teachings offer comfort to those who fear the future. Each age, they stress, unfolds according to a Divine plan and is governed by universal spiritual laws. This final age is also the shortest, lasting for just 2,592 years. The reason for this is that violent, destructive energy swiftly loses its momentum, whereas creative power effects change more steadily. In the early years of the next millennium this season of storms will have run its course and the world will return again to the Krita-yuga, a new Golden Age.

These prophecies are recorded in one of the oldest sacred texts in India, the Vishnu Purana, which also foretells that the Kali-yuga will witness widespread promiscuity and the decline of marriage as an institution, 'The causes of devotion will be confined to physical wellbeing; the only bond between the sexes will be passion ... Marriage will cease being a rite.'

Other images of the twentieth century are evoked elsewhere in the text: 'The only road to success will be the lie. The earth will be honoured for its material treasures only. Those who own and spend more money will be bosses of men who will have only one aim, the gaining of wealth however dishonestly. ... Men will be terrified of death and fear scarcity ...'

The Kali-yuga will produce leaders who 'will be violent and will seize the goods of their subjects. The

*Our present cycle, or Manvantara, is presided over by Kali, the Goddess of Darkness.*

Caste of servants will prevail and the outcasts will rule. Short will be their lives, insatiable their appetites, they will hardly understand the meaning of piety.'

It would be tempting to interpret this passage as predicting the abuse of power by corrupt officals in the medieval Church, the rise of fascist and communist dictatorships in the twentieth century or even the establishment of the bureaucratic system which oils the wheels of power in most modern democracies. All these events fall within the time scale of the current Kali-yuga. In fact, it would be easy to argue a convincing case for any one of innumerable interpretations which accurately reflect the state of chaos and change over the past 2,500 years. It is also tempting to dismiss the predictions as the religious rantings of a priestly caste desperate to denounce the secular delights of the

*The Dark Age will be ruled by outcasts whose lives are fated to be short.*

world they were trying to influence, but is it not more likely that through the concept of the four ages the Hindu prophets wanted also to reveal their insights into the predictable phases and failings of human nature?

The Greek poet and philosopher Hesiod adapted the Hindu teachings into his ideas of the four phases of human development in which the Kali-yuga would correspond to old age. At this time of life a person would be physically and mentally deteriorating, and yet their spirit would have developed though experience and a lifetime of contemplation in preparation for the next

**During this period the earth will also be subject to violent change.**

phase of their spiritual evolution – reincarnation as a more evolved soul. In this context the significance of the millennium would therefore be purely spiritual.

*Sacred Indian texts foretell widespread promiscuity and the decline of marriage in Kali-yuga*

# ANNUS MAGNUS — THE GREAT YEAR

The astrologers, prophets, philosophers and priests of the ancient world regarded the cyclical pattern of the planets as indicative of the cyclical nature of all life on earth. Although each differed in determining the duration of the 'Great Year' - the time the planets took to return to their positions on the day of creation - they all reasoned that it was of enormous significance in predicting future events. Zeno, the Greek philosopher, argued that this signified that history was destined to repeat itself and therefore it was possible to predict events, if not the actual protagonists. The concept has, of course, lost much of its appeal since the discovery of the three outer planets Uranus, Pluto and Neptune.

The cyclical theory of time was defined by the Egyptians using the astronomical concept known as the Precession of the Equinoxes, which is based on the fact that the zodiacal pattern of the planets moves 50.2 seconds in longitude every year in relation to the axis of the earth. The axis takes 25,290 years to complete its rotation, making a reverse circle as it spins. This results in notable dates, such as the Equinox, aligning itself to a different sign of the zodiac every 2,160 years. Consequently, we will not enter the true Age of Aquarius, according to astronomers, until the year 2023, an age when humanity is destined to seek wisdom in preference to knowledge .

# PYRAMID PROPHECIES

**The Great Pyramid at Gizeh symbolizes the mysteries of the ancient world more eloquently than almost any other existing artifact or monument. The accuracy of its construction continues to confound modern architects and engineers, while the discovery of an empty sarcophagus in the King's Chamber has led to speculation as to the pyramid's true purpose.**

*Empty sarcophagi may have been used by the ancient Egyptians for magical purposes, such as projecting the astral body to obtain visions of the future.*

Among the most bizarre theories of modern times are those which aim to prove that the proportions and measurements of the secret chambers and passageways within the pyramid correspond to significant dates in the history of the world, as predicted by the Egyptian priests. Several serious scholars, convinced of the accuracy of these prophecies, have urged us to prepare for the consequences of those relating to the coming millennium.

In the 1925 edition of their book *The Great Pyramid: Its Divine Message,* authors Davidson and Aldersmith, the theory's most adamant exponents, quote an ancient Coptic manuscript in support of their argument. The Great Pyramid, it said, embodies 'the wisdom and aquirements in the different arts and sciences ... that they might remain as records for the benefit of those who would afterwards comprehend them ... the positions of the stars and their cycles, together with the history and chronicle of time past, of that which is to come, and every future event which would take place in Egypt'.

## PIONEERING PYRAMIDOLOGIST

Davidson and Aldersmith were not eccentric Egyptologists, but ardent archaeologists expanding on the theories of the pioneer of pyramid prophecies, Robert Menzies. In 1865, Menzies, a devout Christian, argued that each inch of the passageways corresponded to a solar year, the measurements matching up with Biblical chronology. Consequently the entrance symbolized Creation (which he dated to 4004 BC), the first sloping tunnel represented the Flood and the entrance to the Grand Gallery marked the birth of Christ. The steepness of the Grand Gallery would then signify the ascent of Christian civilization for the next 2000 years, with the doorway of the Antechamber representing the 'last days' as prophesied in the Bible. Remarkably, a controversy subsequently arose not from Menzies's contention that the ancient Egyptians had foretold the coming of Christ, nor even from his dating of the Creation, but from the fact that he had taken the birth of Christ, and not the crucifixion, as marking the beginning of Christianity!

**The pyramid predicts that 'the present evil world' will end in 2874 AD.**

*The enigmatic face of the sphinx which guards the entrance to the Great Pyramid.*

A few years later, fellow Christians John and Morton Edgar went further in trying to establish a mystical significance for each and every structural detail in the pyramid. They made a strong case and the features fell obediently into their allotted place and time – but the brothers failed to convince the archaeological establishment, and just about everyone else, why the ancient Egyptians, with enough gods of their own, would erect a massive monument to a future Messiah. Undaunted, Morton soldiered on alone, deciphering the prophecies he believed were encoded in the pyramid. His calculations led him to conclude that the 'Present Evil World' would run for 6000 years from the Fall of Adam (which he dated to 4126 BC), after which a millennial age would dawn in 1874 with the Final Judgement pencilled in for 2874 AD.

## ACCURATE PREDICTIONS

By the time Davidson and Aldersmith published their conclusions the religious fervour had died down, but intellectual interest in the subject had intensified. Using

the same 'inch for a year' rule, Davidson studied the entire passage system and the proportions of the pyramid to see if the rest of the structure stood up to the same symbolic analysis. It did. For example, he found that the 'Great Step' between The First Ascending Passage and The Grand Gallery corresponded to the 33-year life span of Christ. Further measurements related the 'Time of Tribulation' prophesied in the Bible to the years of the twentieth century and accurately 'predicted' the outbreak and end of World War I. He even drew significance from details such as the narrowing of a passage at a point where it corresponds to the period 1928-36, the years of the Great Depression.

The most remarkable feature of the pyramid prophecies, though, is the fact that having 'proved' the theory to his own satisfaction, Davidson went on to use it to make accurate predictions of events in the future, such as the start of World War II and the dropping of the hydrogen bomb in 1953, rather than merely reinterpreting the past in the light of the theory.

## PYRAMID PREDICTIONS

According to Egyptologist Max Toth, the final message to be decoded from the measurements of the Great Pyramid is that the end of the twentieth century marks the last phase of human history. Toth extended a line from the rear of the King's Chamber to a blind passage, a point which seemed to mark the termination of recorded time according to the ancient architects. According to Toth's calculations, this line corresponds to the years 1992 to 2001, during which a New Age of spiritual enlightenment will emerge. The 'Kingdom of the Spirit' would persist between 1995 and 2025, civilization will begin to break down, and a new social order will be formed, ushered in by signs of the Second Coming. The Messiah will finally appear six years later to initiate a Golden Age of progress and achievement lasting from 2055 to 2080. With the new world order in place, the Messiah will leave the world in 2116, but will return in 2135 and again in 2265, though for what purpose Toth could not predict.

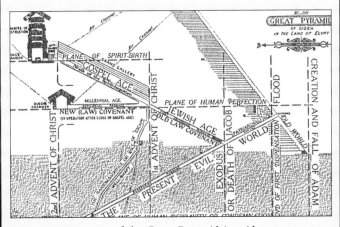

*The passage system of the Great Pyramid is said to represent significant stages in human history.*

# THE APOCALYPTIC PROPHETS OF THE OLD TESTAMENT

**The Old Testament prophets proclaimed a common message, that humanity was doomed to repeat its errors until Armageddon wiped all sin from the world. Such pronouncements were not the manifestos of false messiahs, but were the result of divine inspiration. 'The Lord hath spoken,' proclaimed the prophet Amos, 'who can but prophesy?'**

The biblical prophets were profoundly affected by their visions. Ezekiel would lie in a trance for days afterwards, while Daniel was said to have been violently sick from the emotional strain of the experience. Once they had recovered, their speech was often rambling and confused, their descriptions defying logical interpretation, for words proved inadequate to describe the intensity of their visions.

Yet some of their predictions were explicit, and many appear to have come true. Eight hundred years before Christ, the prophet Isaiah accurately foretold the rise of Babylon, which was then a state of no great importance. Two decades before Babylon invaded the land of Judah and destroyed Jerusalem, the prophet Jeremiah correctly predicted the destruction in considerable detail, adding the fact that the conquered nations would be enslaved by the Babylonians for seventy years until freed by a leader with the name of Cyrus. He was proved correct in every detail.

## THE FALL OF ALEXANDER

Among Daniel's visions are some which appear to foretell the death of Alexander the Great, who died at the height of his power in 323 BC. 'Therefore the he-goat waxed very great: And when he was strong, the great horn was broken; And for it came up four notable ones, toward the four winds of heaven.' These lines could mean almost anything until it is understood that the goat was an accepted symbol of the ancient Greeks. Alexander could then be seen as the 'horn' with the 'four notable ones' symbolizing the four generals who divided the empire after his death.

The accuracy of the prophecies become even harder to deny when those apparently relating the life of Jesus of Nazareth are closely examined. It has been estimated that there are over 300 predictions in the Old Testament relating to the life of Jesus, but of course these concerned the coming

*Both Daniel and King David appear to have predicted the crucifixion of Jesus.*

# THE BOOK OF DANIEL

The Book Of Daniel, the earliest canonical book of prophecy, (written c. 6th century BC) provides a confusion of clues as to the probable date for the end of the world, the likeliest being 2005.

According to the opening chapters, Daniel was one of three Hebrew children who had been enslaved by the Chaldean king Nebuchadnezzar and brought up in the Chaldean capital, Babylon. There he developed a greater 'understanding in all visions and dreams' than the King's own astrologers and priests, culminating in his prediction for the advent and crucifixion of a future messiah.

It is understood that in biblical texts a 'day' is often to be interpreted as the equivalent of a year. Therefore, when Daniel predicts the messiah's arrival as being 'seven weeks, and three score and two weeks' after the rebuilding of the temple in Jerusalem in 457 BC, we can take it as prophesying the advent of a messiah in 30 AD. The number of weeks adds up to 69, or 483 'days', giving the year of 26AD, which then has to be adjusted to take account of the four-year calendar correction of 46BC. More weight is given to the prophecy in a verse which appears to foretell the crucifixion in 33AD and the Jews' dismissal of Jesus as their messiah, 'after threescore and two weeks shall the Messiah be cut off, but not for himself: and (they shall be no more the Messiah's people).'

The Book of Daniel closes with the prophet asking the Almighty, 'How long shall it be to the end of these wonders?' - meaning the end of the world. The Creator enigmatically replies, 'It shall be for a time, times, and a half ... there shall be 1290 days. Blessed is he that waiteth, and cometh to the 1335 days. But go thy way till the end.'

If the start of the apocalyptic clock is taken to be the destruction of the Temple in 70AD, as is commonly believed, the period of 1290 'days' multiplied one and a half times gives the crucial date as 2005AD (1290 plus 645 from 70AD). That year we can expect a second deluge to carry away the sins of the world, 'the end therefore shall be with a flood, and unto the end of the war desolations are determined.' But for the righteous who wait for the 1,335th 'day' (2072AD) immortality is assured.

*The accuracy of Daniel's predictions incurred the anger of Nebuchadnezzar's astrologers and priests.*

*The ruins of Nebuchadnezzar's palace where Daniel perfected his prophetic gifts.*

of an unnamed messiah who would free the Jews, and the Jews refused to accept Jesus as their messiah.

## MIRACLES FORETOLD

Micah named the birthplace of the Messiah, 'the ruler in Israel', as Bethlehem while Ephratah and Isaiah appear to have predicted the miracles: 'Then the eyes of the blind shall be opened, and the ears of the deaf shall be unstopped. Then shall the lame man leap as an hart, and the tongue of the dumb sing'. Or was Isaiah speaking only metaphorically of the joy mankind would feel when the Messiah came?

As for the entrance of Jesus into Jerusalem on the back of a donkey, the detail given in the vision of Zechariah seems very convincing. 'O daughter of Jerusalem: behold, the king cometh unto thee: he is just, and having salvation; lowly, and riding upon an ass.' Speaking in the first person, Zechariah even predicts the exact price of Judas' betrayal: 'So they weighed for my price thirty pieces of silver.'

**There were over 300 predictions in the Old Testament foretelling the life of Jesus.**

And yet it was not a prophet who appears to have foretold the terrible climax of the drama, the crucifixion, but the Hebrews' greatest ruler, King David. A thousand years before the birth of Jesus he dreamt of a method of execution which had yet to be devised by the Romans: 'they pierced my hands and my feet. I may tell all my bones: they look and stare upon me. They part my garments among them, and cast lots upon my vesture.'

# PROPHECIES OF THE LAST DAYS

**The prophets of the Old Testament were primarily religious teachers whose purpose was to communicate God's will to his chosen people. For them, the true purpose of prophecy was not to foretell the future, but to reveal the hidden wonders of God.**

*In the esoteric tradition it is accepted that the Biblical prophets were speaking metaphorically of building a New Jerusalem within each individual.*

Many Biblical scholars believe that we are now living in the 'last days', the final years of human history before Armageddon. They claim that the apocalyptic clock began ticking on 14 May 1948, the day the state of Israel was founded, as the return of the Hebrew tribes to Palestine was a precondition for the Second Coming of Christ. They cite the prophecies recorded in Deuteronomy which foretold the dispersal and persecution of the Jews: 'And the Lord shall scatter thee among all people, from one end of the earth unto the other.' They also quote the prophecy of Ezekiel which recorded God's promise to help the Jews to return to their homeland once they had submitted to his will: 'For I will take you from among the heathen, and gather you out of all countries, and will bring you into your own land.'

Ezekiel went on to describe the rejuvenation of the desolate desert of Palestine – which is exactly what the modern Israelis have accomplished – and he predicted that

Israel would be besieged by an army from the north (which he called Gog) aided by their allies from Persia, Ethiopia and Libya. Israel will then be caught in a pincer movement by armies from the north and south at the same moment as the invaders attack Egypt. There was indeed a clash of arms between Russia and Egypt during the premiership of Egypt's President Anwar El Sadat and there have been numerous attacks on Israel by its Arab neighbours since then, but on each occasion the conflict has been contained.

**Many Biblical scholars believe that we are now living in the 'last days'.**

According to Ezekiel the final attack by the armies from the north will be repulsed not by the Israeli military machine, but by divine intervention. 'At the same time when Gog shall come against the land of Israel there shall be a great shaking in the land, the mountains shall be thrown down, and the steep places shall fall, and every wall shall fall to the ground.' Some have interpreted this passage as a vision of a last-ditch nuclear strike by the Israelis, but the Biblical prophets would not have conceived of such destruction as being anything other than the wrath of God. In their world men were limited to swords and arrows. Only God could vent his displeasure on such a massive scale.

## NATURAL DISASTERS

According to Zechariah, a series of natural disasters will pursue the fleeing invaders back to their own lands, where a plague will wither their flesh from their bones before the entire earth is engulfed in flames. Of the survivors, Micah says, 'they shall beat their swords into ploughshares, and their spears into pruning hooks: nation shall not lift up a sword against nation, neither shall they learn war anymore.'

Most political commentators agree that, despite recent moves towards a permanent peace, the Middle East

*According to the Biblical prophets, Armageddon will be ignited by violence in the Middle East.*

remains a volatile area. If World War III were to break out, it is conceivable that it would be triggered in this region. For Israel and the West the threat from Iran (Persia) and Libya remains very real, but Ethiopia has never been an enemy of Israel and the fall of communism has dispelled the prospect of a war with Russia. Moreover, the prophets speak in terms of armies wielding swords and riding horses, a description which could not apply to any modern army. So, are we mistaken to interpret Biblical prophecies as foretelling future events? Should we dismiss them instead as mere myth and superstition, or interpret them as veiled insights into the perennial paradox of the human personality?

## THE HEBREW MILLENNIUM

Jewish mythology refuses to put a date on the End of the World, but states that after the final conflagration Israel's enemies will be punished for having persecuted the Chosen People, while the righteous will be allowed to enter a new Garden of Eden. However, some Talmudic scholars contend that the end will not be violent, but rather that everything will simply return to its source - the Creator.

The only clue to the date of this final year is the Hebrew belief in a cycle of seven ages, each of which is said to be symbolic of a stage in the spiritual evolution of the universe and is said to last seven thousand years. Seven is a sacred number in the Jewish calendar. It symbolizes 'wholeness' or 'harmony', and multiples of

seven govern all the major religious festivals. The End of the World is said to begin after seven cycles of seven thousand years have passed. In the Jewish calendar 2000 AD will be 5760 so the End of the World looks likely for the year 43240 AD.

According to the *Temunah*, an anonymous Jewish work of the thirteenth century, we are currently living at the end of the first cycle in an age characterized by the struggle between the materialistic and the spiritual. The new millennium will mark the end of that age and will be a sabbatical 'year' lasting a thousand years of earthly time. The next age will begin in the year 3240 AD and will be a Golden Age, an era of peace and tranquillity.

# JESUS — THE PACIFIST PROPHET

**According to the Gospels, Jesus saw his life and crucifixion as fulfilling the predictions of the Old Testament prophets. St Luke quotes him as saying, 'All things must be fulfilled, which were written in the law of Moses, and in the prophets, and in the psalms, concerning me.' But were the prophecies perverted to fit early Church propaganda?**

The Apostles wrote the Gospels not only because they wanted to record the teachings of Jesus, but also because they were eager to prove that Jesus had fulfilled all the ancient prophecies concerning the coming of the Messiah. They cite his persecution by those who did not want to hear his message in an attempt to invite comparison with the prophets of ancient times.

After the crucifixion the Apostles disagreed over their interpretations of the teachings of Jesus and went their separate ways. Each Gospel is a mass of contradictions and conflicting doctrine, portraying Christ alternately as the unforgiving instrument of God's wrath ('I have come to bring fire on the earth') and as the prophet of compassion, encouraging his followers to 'turn the other cheek'. What are we then to make of the predictions attributed to him in the 'official' canonical Gospels?

*The Apostles differed radically in their descriptions of Jesus and attributed teachings to him which are clearly contradictory.*

## WAR AND FAMINE

St Mark claims that Jesus predicted a series of wars in the final years before Armageddon: 'Wars must come, but the end won't follow immediately. For nation shall rise against nation and kingdom against kingdom, and there will be great earthquakes, and famines in many lands, and epidemics, and terrifying things happening in the heavens.' Whether or not these words were actually spoken by Jesus, the inclusion of this warning of impending apocalypse in the Gospels was surely intended to stimulate recruitment into the early Church and fortify the resolve of those who were waivering from the faith under Roman persecution.

According to Matthew, we must accept the end, however it comes, as inevitable, 'And accept those days should be shortened, there should no flesh be saved: but for the elect's sake those days shall be shortened.' But if Jesus had proclaimed fire and damnation in the manner of the ancients, might he really have been referring to the end of the world, or only to the end of our own personal world, our death when we leave the world of flesh for the world of pure spirit? If so, the 'elect' he refers to could then be interpreted as being the first of a new race of more highly developed human beings who will evolve only after mankind has made the necessary leap in consciousness from a materialistic to a spiritual view of existence.

## DIVINE DESTINY

A further hint of our divine destiny might be gleaned from a passage in Luke which appears to speak of the current decline in orthodox religion and the fear of those with nothing but blind faith to guide them when this greater reality begins to dawn. 'And there shall be signs in the sun, and in the moon, and in the stars; and upon the earth distress of nations, with perplexity; the sea and the waves roaring; men's hearts failing them for fear, and for looking after those things which are coming on the earth: for the powers of heaven shall be shaken.' The traditional interpretation of this passage sees it as yet another series of natural disasters provoked by God's frustration with a sinful world, but if, as Jesus himself said, God is Love and should be envisaged as our benign Heavenly Father, why would He destroy His creation in a fit of pique, no matter how frustrated He might be with us? Is it not more likely that the early Church fathers selectively edited the text to portray Jesus as an apocalyptic prophet because as such he would make more persuasive propaganda for a Church that was intent on setting itself up as the authorized mediator

**The early Church selectively edited the Gospels for their own ends.**

*The Church assumed the role of authorized mediator between man and God.*

between man and God? And could it not be, as the recently recovered Gnostic Gospel of Thomas suggests (see box), that Jesus actually preached a doctrine of love so that humanity would awaken to its own divine potential, warning only of what we might bring upon ourselves, in the form of arrested spiritual development, by living in the darkness of ignorance?

# WHAT THE 'LOST' GOSPEL TELLS US

In 1945 a complete Coptic text of a 'lost' Gospel, The Gospel of Thomas, was discovered in caves at Nag Hammadi in Upper Egypt. Prior to this discovery it was thought that all copies of the Gospel had been destroyed on the orders of the Church on the pretext that it was heretical. On closer study, Thomas' Gospel certainly does not conform to the orthodox view of Jesus as Christ, the Messiah, the Son of God. There is no mention of his virgin birth, of the 'miracles', the crucifixion or the resurrection. Instead it simply records what the anonymous author claims are the sayings of Jesus without any further commentary or attempt at interpretation.

In contrast to the 'official' Gospels, Jesus does not prophesy an apocalypse prior to the establishment of God's kingdom on earth, but remarks that 'the new world' is already here. 'What you look for has come, but you do not know it.' The inference is that we are so wrapped up in ourselves that we cannot experience it. The sayings repeatedly stress that 'the kingdom of God' resides within each of us and not in a mythical heaven to which the 'sinner' will be denied admittance. This 'message' further undermines the authority of the established Church.

Towards the end, Jesus warns against entrusting one's spiritual development to others, be they prophets, politicians or priests!
'If those who guide your Being say to you: "Behold the Kingdom is in the Heaven,"
then the birds of the sky will precede you.
If they say to you: "It is in the sea", then the fish will precede you.
But the Kingdom is in your centre. And is about you.
When you know your Selves then you will be known
and you will be aware that you are the sons of the Living Father.
But if you do not know yourselves then you are in poverty, and you are the poverty.'
From the study of the manuscript and other Gnostic texts, it appears that there were two opposing groups of early Christians, one eager to present Jesus as a simple holy man and the other desperate to adopt him as an apocalyptic saviour. The latter sect apparently succeeded in suppressing the former and went on to found the early Church.

# THE 'LOST' APOCALYPSE

**The word 'apocalypse' has come to mean a future time of cataclysm and divine retribution, although its original meaning was 'to reveal' or 'disclose' spiritual knowledge through the gift of prophecy. The recent discovery of the Nag Hammadi manuscripts, containing what appear to be the original apocalyptic gospels of the early Christians, is now forcing the Church to re-examine the origins of Christianity and the true meaning of the Apocalypse.**

*In the Gnostic Apocalypse of St Peter the Apostle has a vision of Christ's astral body at the crucifixion.*

The Nag Hammadi manuscripts are all that remains of a secret library of sacred and esoteric texts collected by a diverse group of early ascetic Christian sects known collectively as the Gnostics, from the Greek word *gnosis*, meaning 'knowledge'. While each group developed its own ethics and theology, some of which were quite radical, they all shared the belief that the future of humanity depended on its search for secret knowledge, and not on wholesale salvation through a messiah. Faith, they argued, was not enough. Consequently they were persecuted by the orthodox Church, who regarded them as a threat to its authority.

Nevertheless the Church was forced to assimilate some Gnostic doctrine because it had been taught by a number of the Apostles and it made sound spiritual sense. There were political reasons too. The early Church Fathers wanted to appease their Greek and Jewish converts – the two traditions which were at the source of gnostic teachings – but they were equally keen to distance themselves from the more mystical aspects of these traditions. St Peter and Saul of Tarsus (St Paul) were just two of several Gnostic Apostles whose teachings were selectively edited by the early Church in an attempt to remove all references to direct individual spiritual experience such as reincarnation and astral projection.

In the Gnostic Apocalypse of St Peter the Apostle recalls meeting Jesus 'in the spirit' and being stoned by priests who wanted to suppress his teachings. A subsequent passage describes St Peter's vision of seeing the spirit, or astral body, of Jesus at the crucifixion and of being told that it is only his body which is suffering. His true essence cannot die and this knowledge, later misinterpreted by the Church as promising a resurrection in the flesh, must be shared with all initiates to the new religion. Peter asked the spirit of Jesus, 'Who is this one glad and laughing on the tree (cross)? And is it another one whose feet and hands they are striking?' Jesus says, 'He whom you saw on the tree, glad and laughing, this is the living Jesus. But this one into whose hands and feet they drive the nails is the fleshy part, which is the substitute being put to shame, the one who came into being in his likeliness. But look at him and me.' Jesus appeared to foresee the suppression and misinterpretation of his teachings for he told St Peter, "These things, then, which you saw you shall present to those of another race who are not of this age."

## ASTRAL TRAVELS

In the Gnostic 'Apocalypse of St Paul' the Apostle describes in great detail leaving his body and ascending to the third heaven accompanied by a guiding spirit. He is told by the spirit to look back to where his body lies so that he will not dismiss the experience as a dream. When he reaches the fourth level he sees another soul returning to the world to be reincarnated. 'The soul that had been cast down [went] to [a] body which had been prepared.'

*The Church has traditionally portrayed St Peter and St Paul as mere messengers and disciples of Jesus.*

# ESCHATOLOGY

Eschatology is the body of orthodox Christian doctrine concerning life after death and the end of the world.

The concept of physical resurrection was adopted by the early Christians as a reward for the righteous. From this grew the idea of an 'end time' when all believers would be recalled to life from the grave by Christ the Messiah who will return to earth to resurrect the righteous in the flesh and reign over them for one thousand years. In the final year of this millennium, all will be judged: the righteous will ascend to heaven and the impure souls cast down into eternal damnation.

Fear of this Day of Judgement gave impetus to recruitment for the early Church and also fuelled its Fundamentalist movements from the Middle Ages to the present day. The Seventh-Day Adventists, for example, state categorically in Article 10 of their 'Fundamental Beliefs' that 'The condition of man in death is one of unconsciousness. That all men, good and evil alike, remain in the grave from death to the resurrection.' But the physical resurrection is not consistent with the teachings of St Paul and St Peter.

*The esoteric practice of ascending in the spirit to the higher realms was corrupted in the concept of the Last Judgement.*

The Gnostics believed that each individual's experience after death depended on the knowledge he or she had gained of the higher worlds through study or travelling 'in the spirit' during meditation. However, only fragments of these suppressed teachings are to be found in the 'official' Gospels, while those relating to reincarnation were excised by the Church in 553 AD.

The concept of travelling in the astral, or spirit body, which St Paul, being a Cabbalist, would have practised, is referred to only fleetingly, as in *Corinthians* where he describes a state of exaltation as 'such as one caught up to the third heaven'. Later he recalls, 'I knew a man in Christ [ie, a Christian convert] above fourteen years ago (whether in the body, I cannot tell; or whether out of the body, I cannot tell: God knoweth).'

> Only fragments of these suppressed teachings are to be found in the 'official' Gospels.

The Greek Cabbalist and Gnostic philosopher Philo of Alexandria (circa 20BC–50AD), whose concept of the 'Word' was later incorporated into the Gospel of St John, also wrote of travelling 'in the spirit'. He envisaged a ladder of 'Names stretching from Earth to Heaven' with each level guarded by beings who will only admit the traveller if that traveller has the spiritual knowledge to gain from the experience.

This suppression of the mystical tradition which the early Church inherited from its founders and their converts has brought it into conflict with those seeking the true 'gnosis' of Christianity. Revealing these spiritual truths and teachings could be said to be the real meaning of the Apocalypse.

# THE APOCALYPSE OF ST JOHN

The graphic imagery contained in the Book of Revelation, often referred to as the Apocalypse of St John, and the dire warnings it proclaims have been a source of inspiration and speculation for millions of Christians and non-Christians alike for almost two thousand years. And yet now, as we approach the new millennium, an epoch which many believe to be that which St John prophesied for the final battle between Good and Evil, serious doubts are being cast on the authorship, origin and traditional interpretation of this part of the Bible.

*The Four Horsemen of the Apocalypse – bringers of War, Famine, Death and Disease – are traditionally interpreted as the embodiments of God's wrath.*

If these recent theories are proved to be correct (see pages 26-27) they would almost certainly invalidate the year 2000 AD as the likeliest date for Armageddon, but may instead reveal a previously hidden mystical meaning behind the visions John describes.

Whoever the true author (or authors) of the Book of Revelation might be, their prime purpose was to rekindle religious fervour in the followers of Jesus who, at that time were suffering persecution under the emperors Nero (54-68 AD) and Domitian (81-96 AD).

The first two chapters of Revelation are taken up with St John's letter to the seven Churches of Asia, urging them not to lose faith, while the middle section contains a detailed description of the vision. In Chapter 3 St John leaves his body and enters heaven 'in the spirit'. As he ascends he hears a distant voice calling to him in the rasping tone of a trumpet. He looks up to see a God-like figure surrounded by an aura in all the colours of the rainbow. The figure is seated on a throne in front of which sit the heavenly court, seven spirits of God (seven being the mystical number of perfection or wholeness), and 24 crowned elders with 'thousands and thousands' of angels in attendance. Before them lie four creatures which are similar to those seen by Ezekiel, the Old Testament prophet – a lion, a calf, an eagle and a man. In St John's vision, each of these beasts has six wings and many eyes. The figure holds a book in one hand, a book with seven seals which no mortal man can open, but which a slain lamb with seven horns and seven eyes (symbolic of Christ) opens for him. With the opening of each seal the wrath of God is unleashed on the world in various forms.

## THE HORSEMEN

In breaking the first four seals the Four Horsemen of the Apocalypse are unleashed: the first is white, symbolizing War (but also Victory and Purity); the second red, symbolizing Hunger (but also violence, wealth and debauchery – ie, spiritual hunger); the third black, symbolizing Suffering (but also death); and the fourth green, symbolizing Disease (also decay). With the opening of the fifth seal, the murdered martyrs call for revenge, and with the sixth, the world is rocked by a mighty earthquake. The opening of the seventh seal brings a silence in heaven.

**The prime purpose of the authors of Revelation was to rekindle religious fervour in the followers of Christ who were suffering persecution.**

Seven angels then blow in turn upon seven trumpets, each signalling a new plague upon the earth. The first brings hail and fire to lay waste to a third of the earth's surface. The second brings a volcano crashing into the sea, turning a third of the waters to blood. It also causes a star to fall from the sky, turning the river waters bitter. With the fourth trumpet a third of the moon, the sun and the stars go dark, while the fifth trumpet blast brings a plague of locusts to all who do not bear the mark of God on their foreheads. The sixth trumpet calls two hundred million angels on horseback to slay a third of mankind.

At this point, an angel appears holding a small book, roars like a lion and then feeds the book to St John. He describes it as tasting as sweet as honey but filling his stomach with bitterness. It apparently inspires him to make a lengthy proclamation concerning the various nations of the earth after which two witnesses are then sent to earth, are killed by a creature referred to as 'the Beast', but are then brought back to life by God. The most dramatic portion of the apocalypse then closes with the sounding of the seventh trumpet, heralding the Last Judgement for the 'quick and the dead'.

*Did St John foresee the extent of industrial pollution in the modern world?*

## SEALS AND SYMBOLISM

In recent years new interpretations have been offered as to the meaning behind the imagery in St John's Revelation.

The image 'the heaven was removed as a scroll when it is rolled up' is now being read as an accurate prediction of the erosion of the ozone layer. In another passage a star of heaven called 'Wormwood' falls to earth and poisons the rivers. This had long been accepted as foretelling the fall of a meteorite, but since 1945 it has taken on an even more sinister significance – that man may now bring about his own destruction through atomic warfare. Wormwood is said to open a 'bottomless pit', releasing the armies of the angel Abaddon which take the forms of locusts with human features. It is these beings which Charles Manson is said to have hoped to invoke through the blood letting of the Hollywood murders.

The final predictions are still open to innumerable interpretations. St John saw seven angels emptying the contents of seven vials over mankind. The first infects the followers of the Beast with a plague of sores, the second kills all forms of marine life, the third turns the rivers to blood, the fourth magnifies the power of the sun to burn mankind, the fifth darkens the kingdom of the Beast and the sixth dries the Euphrates River, allowing the East to invade Israel and then Europe. Many see this as prophesying that Islamic Fundamentalists will conquer the West – a vision shared by the medieval seer Nostradamus. The emptying of the final vial will poison the atmosphere wiping out the rest of humanity.

*A late medieval depiction of the Four Horsemen.*

# THE REVELATION OF ST JOHN

**St John's vision of the Apocalypse, as detailed in the Book of Revelation, has been a foundation of Christian philosophy and faith for almost two thousand years. It is the source of Christian belief in the Second Coming of Christ and the millennial paradise that will follow. But its authorship and origin have always been controversial.**

St John is said to have written the Book of Revelation on the island of Patmos in the eastern Aegean during the first century AD. The location could be the first clue to the book's true origin, a trail which appears to lead to a very different source from that accepted by the Church.

Patmos was a close neighbour of the major Greek trading city of Ephesus, which was then a centre of pagan culture and a reservoir of the esoteric teachings that had trickled from the tributaries of Egypt and Chaldea. A closer examination of the contents and style of the work suggests that although its framing chapters are undoubtedly Christian in character, the core of the book and its prophecies might be a compilation of Jewish, Egyptian and Greek mystical lore which would have been in circulation in the city at the time. Its substance might even have originated in the sacred texts of the Eleusinian or Phrygian mystery cults.

The mythical beasts which St John conjures up to plague the world are mostly drawn from the mythology of the

*The symbolism of Revelation might hide secrets of the Eleusinian mystery religions.*

ancient Egyptians, while the grammar is typical of the Old Testament. So too are the key symbols of the lamb as representing the king of Israel (from the Book of Enoch) and the four horsemen (from Zechariah). It could further be argued that the early Christians adopted the symbol of the lamb as an appropriate emblem of the sacrificial Christ from the pagans, who had long used lambs as sacrificial offerings.

## APOCALYPTIC PLAGUES

The apocalyptic plagues recall those described in Exodus as preceding the Jews' flight from Egypt, while the obligatory elements accompanying God's show of displeasure are a familiar feature from the books of Isaiah, Ezekiel, Joel and Amos. Even the number of the righteous quoted by St John appears to have been taken from Old Testament sources. 144,000 was the number arrived at by multiplying the twelve tribes of Israel by the twelve priests who led them and again by the symbolic figure of one thousand, which represented the community.

The central segment of the Book of Revelation, which describes the prophet's vision of the throne of

*St John's apocalyptic vision records a glimpse of cosmic mysteries.*

## EARLY INTERPRETATIONS

The first century scholar St Jerome, who translated many of the Gospels from Greek to Latin, declared that the Revelation of St John was open to seven equally valid and illuminating interpretations. Later, in the fourth century AD, St Augustine considered it to be an allegory of spiritual truths and declared that the millennium had begun with the crucifixion. Certainly when it is viewed as a revelationary text in the tradition of true prophecy, it begins to make a lot more sense.

In the first chapter St John describes a radiant, robed being in the likeness of a man. Dr Rudolf Steiner, founder of the Anthroposophical Society, saw this being as the archetype of human evolution: 'The beginning of earthly evolution stands forth in the fiery feet, its end in the fiery countenance, and the complete power of the "creative word", to be finally won, is seen in the fiery source coming out of the mouth.'

Even St John's discourses to the seven churches of Asia can be accorded mystical significance if they are read as signifying the prophet's meditation on the seven major chakras or sacred energy centres of the etheric body, the seven 'churches' of the spirit. In the Western esoteric tradition the four horsemen of the apocalypse stand instead for the four stages of individual human development - birth, youth, maturity and death - while in the East they have long symbolized the four yugas, or epochs, of the world. Wormwood, the falling star, is said to symbolize the way that these and other items of secret knowledge were once misused by man, as a result of which they were hidden from view for each man to search out anew for himself.

heaven and the opening of the seven seals, is strikingly similar to the Hebrew apocalyptic texts, but it has been peppered with key phrases that are characteristic of Christian literature which seem artificial in this context. The contention is that a Christian editor has added his comments at a later date to bring it into line with contemporary Church doctrine.

Moreover, the content and style of the framing chapters are not consistent with the other Gospels, suggesting that these might have been the work not of the Apostle John, as traditionally believed, but of a new Christian convert, possibly a Jewish-born evangelical baptist whose work was appropriated by the Church simply because its themes coincided with the beliefs of the editors. He may even have been an initiate of the Greek Mystery religions. This would explain why the true meaning of the vision is deliberately obscured by symbolism. As an initiate he would have been prohibited from recording their teachings in detail. In fact, it is very unlikely that Revelation is the work of one author because the writing suggests a prolonged period of selective editing and enforced enlargements.

It was clearly the intention of the editor (or editors) to reconcile early Christian doctrine with popular pagan beliefs, and to compile all the earlier apocalyptic motifs and themes into one dramatic narrative. The value of the work for the modern reader therefore is not to be found in the book's predictions, for there are none, but in its symbols which offer a glimpse behind the curtain veiling the Cosmic Mysteries.

'Blessed is he that readeth, and they that hear the words of this prophecy, and keep those things that are written therein: for the time is at hand.'

# FALSE PROPHETS AND MAD MESSIAHS

From Biblical times to the present day apocalyptic prophets and self-appointed messiahs have attracted, deceived and corrupted hundreds of thousands of willing followers around the world, despite the fact that all who proclaimed a Second Coming and the End of the World have, so far, been proved wrong.

Theirs is a dualistic world, a world polarized into Good and Evil. They often promise to create a haven for their disillusioned disciples who they have brainwashed into believing that the outside world is godless, evil and corrupt. And yet, ironically, their actions are more characteristic of the Antichrist whom they claim to be saving their followers from. In assuming the role of a Saviour, demanding rather than earning obedience and respect, the false prophet and mad messiah becomes inhuman, anti-social and often immoral – a real Anti-Christ.

Charles Manson and David Koresh assumed the role of what Freud called 'the dreaded primal father', offering their acolytes a false refuge from reality and responsibility. Others such as Shoko Asahara were revealed as fake gurus who exploited their disciples' hunger for a meaning in life, while Adolf Hitler mesmerized millions by focusing their paranoia and prejudices.

We would all like to think that we could never be taken in by such transparent manipulation, but all of these fanatics and opportunists exploited basic human failings and desires which are common, to one degree or another, in all of us. The unpalatable fact is that they would not have been able to initiate their own personal apocalypse had there not been so many 'ordinary' people willing to entrust them with their lives.

# THE MESSIAHS OF THE FIRST MILLENNIUM

**After the crucifixion of Jesus of Nazareth the Jews of Palestine lost their enthusiasm for heaven-sent Sons of God and instead put their faith in flesh-and-blood leaders. Under these millennial prophets and would-be messiahs the downtrodden and disaffected masses believed they could storm the citadels of their oppressors and establish the new millennium by force rather than faith.**

imon Bar Kochba, a Judaean guerrilla leader who died while leading a failed armed revolt against the Roman occupiers in 132 AD, had only accepted the title of 'messiah' to appease the oppressed people who needed to believe in him. His inevitable defeat after three bloody years of fighting, in which half a million Jews died, forced Jews the world over to accept their fate from then on with quiet resignation.

The yearning to return to Jerusalem remained, however, for those in distant lands. 300 years after Bar Kochba's defeat, a would-be messiah, whose name history does not record, went among the Jewish community in Crete promising to part the sea and lead all who would follow him back to the Promised Land.

Incredibly, hundreds rushed home to pack their belongings and then waited patiently on the seashore. The new 'Moses' dutifully appeared and ordered the faithful to stride into the sea while with signs and passes he commanded the waters to part. In their enthusiasm dozens were drowned while their messiah made his escape in the confusion.

In 720 AD, Serene, a Syrian, succeeded in convincing hundreds of disaffected Jews in France and Spain that he would bring them back to Palestine and return to them the land of their forefathers, land that they considered had been taken from them by the conquering Muslims. Naturally, the Muslims were unwilling to hand it over and ordered Serene's arrest.

To everyone's surprise the Caliph, Yazid II, viewed Serene's crusade with compassion and turned him over to the rabbis for trial. They in turn were lenient. They admonished him and his followers, whipped a few of the

*The mythic figure of Christ had no impact on the Jews of the first millennium who still prayed for the appearance of their own messiah.*

ring leaders, confiscated their possessions and made them swear an oath in the synagogue not to upset their Muslim neighbours again.

Serene's 'successor', the Persian sect leader Abu Isa Isfahani, did not get off so lightly. In 750 AD Isfahani abandoned his work as a tailor to take on the might of Islam. Adopting the title 'The Fifth and Last Messenger of the Messiah', he formed an army to speed the approach of the End of Days which would see the dispersal of the Gentiles from the Holy Land, the return of the Jews to Jerusalem and the arrival of the Messiah.

**Simon Bar Kochba had only accepted the title of 'messiah' to appease the oppressed people who needed to believe in him.**

Although illiterate himself, Isfahani encouraged his followers to study the Koran and the Gospels, because these contained the teachings of Jesus and Mohammed, whom he considered to be God's prophets. However, these concessions were not sufficient to placate the Caliph. After a prolonged and bloody campaign, which lasted until 755 AD, Isfahani and his army were defeated.

Although it is almost certain that the one-time tailor met his end in the final battle, the faith of his followers could not be shaken by mere facts. They persisted in their belief that he had survived by drawing a magic circle around himself and then quietly disappearing when the dust had settled!

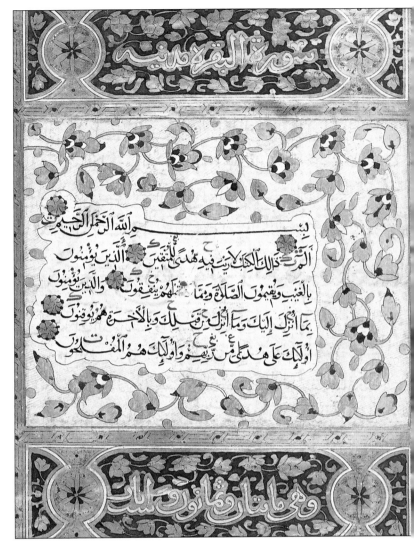

*Isfahani, 'The Fifth and Last Messenger of the Messiah', encouraged his followers to study the Koran and the Gospels.*

# TANCHELM

Tanchelm, a minor Belgian court official, was the first would-be messiah of the second millennium, although he had begun modestly enough, by proclaiming himself the prophet of the underprivileged.

In 1110, after his expulsion from Bruges for publicly predicting the downfall of the Church, he wandered the countryside of Flanders in the simple habit of a monk, setting up his pulpit in the squares and market places, from where he spoke out against the hypocrisy and excesses of the clergy.

The Church, he proclaimed, was corrupt and the priests so steeped in sin that they were unfit to administer the sacraments or grant absolution to ordinary people. Consequently, it was the moral duty of the populace to refuse to pay the annual tithes, or taxes, to the Church authorities.

Tanchelm's conclusion made him very popular with the peasants and before long he had amassed a sizeable following, a personal bodyguard of 3000 men and all the gilded regalia befitting a pretender to the throne. But far from abolishing the tithes, whenever Tanchelm's associates took over a church they simply appropriated them to fund the prophet's campaign.

Intoxicated with power Tanchelm proclaimed himself to be Divine, the incarnation of the Holy Spirit, gathering about him twelve loyal apostles and a mistress he called the Virgin Mary. At one point he conducted a bizarre betrothal ceremony in which he promised himself to a statue of the Virgin. Although he had begun as a prophet of the poor, at the height of his ministry Tanchelm was being lauded as the new Christ by the merchant classes who showered him with jewellery and hard cash. Many paid to drink his bathwater in a ritual which perverted the partaking of the sacrament. This act so incensed one belligerent priest that he risked eternal damnation by murdering Tanchelm, thus robbing the movement of its messiah.

# ANABAPTISTS: TOO MANY PROPHETS

**Many false prophets and would-be messiahs have justified their own paranoia and the isolationist policy of their movements by inventing a threat from the outside world. The German Anabaptists had no need for conspiracy theories. In 1534 they were literally besieged by the Bishop of Münster, who considered them the army of the Antichrist.**

*A medieval woodcut depicting the popular view of the extremism associated with the Anabaptists*

The movement had begun in Zürich around 1523 as a peaceful, though vehemently anti-Catholic, Christian brotherhood. The name Anabaptist derived from the movement's central tenet, an opposition to infant baptism. However, a more contentious issue was their assertion that faith alone would bring each man to God without the intercession of the Church.

Inevitably, this brought the Anabaptists into conflict with the Church authorities, who, in 1527, successfully petitioned Archduke Ferdinand of Austria to condemn the movement by exaggerating the threat it posed. They argued that the Anabaptists were founded on false prophecy, or 'inner revelation', and had degenerated into a heretical cult.

Hans Hut, a disciple of Thomas Müntzer, had been the first of a whole flock of prophets to whip up the sect's latent hostility towards the Church authorities and their supporters among their nobility. He had predicted the Second Coming of Christ for the year 1528, when the Messiah would return to authorize the slaughter of the priests for perverting His teachings and to inaugurate an era of free love and the communal sharing of property. However, Hut was imprisoned and executed together with many of his followers before the Messiah could intervene to save him.

In the following months women and young girls suspected of belonging to the movement were ordered to be publicly drowned in village ponds throughout Austria, and entire Anabaptist communities were burned alive inside their meeting houses.

Prior to these persecutions the brotherhood had believed that one day they would be called by God to fight the forces of darkness in preparation for the Second Coming. That day, they regretfully concluded, had arrived. In moving against them the authorities were unwittingly fulfilling the prophecies of the movement's leaders, justifying their fears and fuelling their paranoia. Now the sect members saw themselves as the 'elect', spoken of in the Book of Revelation, and their persecution as the 'messianic woes' which were to be the birth pangs of the Millennium.

This religious fervour was fanned by an itinerant prophet and visionary, Melchior Hoffmann, who joined the movement in 1529 in order to broadcast his favourite prediction that the Millennium would begin in 1533, fifteen hundred years after the crucifixion. The following year, still raving that he would be proved right, Hoffmann was captured and caged in a tower from which only death would eventually free him.

## RIGHTEOUS REVOLUTION

His successor was prophet Jan Matthyson, a militant Dutch radical who wanted to lead a revolution of the righteous to bring about the Millennium by force. Matthyson and his protégé, Jan Bockelson, were seen by the movement as reincarnations of the Biblical prophets Enoch and Elijah whose reappearance, it was believed, signalled the End of Days.

After Matthyson had proclaimed the German town of Münster to be the site of the New Jerusalem, thousands of Anabaptists swarmed into the city. Along with them came the idle and the indolent, 'fugitives, exiles and criminals', according to a contemporary source, and those who despised the clergy for their wealth and not their beliefs. The number of believers came to outnumber the citizens, most of whom were hounded out of the city by these 'Children of God', and left to beg or die of starvation.

Prince-Bishop Francis von Waldeck, the city's nominal ruler responded by putting the city under a blockade, but somehow Matthyson and his wife, an ex-nun, slipped in unseen. Once inside, they announced their arrival in spectacular fashion; Mattyson, tall and handsome, with a dark beard, wore Biblical robes and carried aloft two stone tablets inscribed with divine dictation.

In the following days Matthyson the robed prophet, and Bockelson, his equally striking administrator, were said to have moved the Münster women in ways which were decidedly secular. 'The madness of the pagan bacchantes cannot have surpassed that of these women,' wrote a contemporary witness. '[some] ran about almost naked, without the least sense of shame; others again flung themselves on the ground with arms extended in the shape of a cross; then rose, clapped their hands, knelt down and cried, grinding their teeth, foaming at the mouth, beating their breasts, weeping, laughing, howling, and uttering the most strange, inarticulate sounds.'

> Mattyson and Bockelson were said to have moved the Münster women in ways which were decidedly secular.

The line between religious fervour and fanaticism became blurred. Matthyson assumed the role of dictator, introducing a reign of terror in which summary executions became a daily occurrence. The city's libraries were sacked and the books burned by hysterical mobs delighting in their illiteracy. Matthyson's madness finally drove him to a last desperate act. After what amounted to a dramatically staged Last Supper, he and twenty of his 'apostles' left the safety of the city to make a suicidal assault on the Bishop's troops. All were killed.

Bockelson then took command, promising his people that God would send another, even greater prophet, and that they, His Chosen People, were only to hold out until the Messiah relieved them. In the meantime he married the first of sixteen wives, Matthyson's widow.

Towards the end of the year-long siege the starving survivors were reported to have been reduced to devouring the corpses of their brethren, and still they remained faithful to, or in fear of, their messiah. Eventually Bockelson was betrayed; four of his followers fled to the Bishop with plans of the city's defences. The city was swiftly overrun and the survivors ruthlessly slaughtered. Bockelson was tried and publicly executed, his flesh burned with hot pincers, his heart pierced with a heated dagger and his tongue cut out as the Bishop looked on.

# ONE FLOCK, ONE KING

The Anabaptist movement gave Jan Bockelson, a former tailor, bankrupt and aimless wanderer, a mission in life. If he could not be a success in the real world, he reasoned, he would at least act the part to the hilt on the stage which Matthyson had set for him. Bockelson had first appeared before the Münster Anabaptists carrying a staff and dressed in the robes of a biblical prophet, but after his mentor's death he proclaimed himself King of the New Zion, a title he claimed to have taken on with some reluctance. In Münster the prophecies of the Old Testament foretelling 'One sheep-fold, one flock, one King', were to be realized and from there spread out to encompass the world. Bockelson wasted no time in ordering a goldsmith to fashion not one but two crowns to commemorate the occasion together with a golden chain of office, a gold sceptre, a golden scabbard for his bejewelled sword and rings for himself and his queen. He commandeered the most magnificent mansion in Münster as his palace and installed his sixteen wives in the house next door.

While his followers were required by royal decree to be modest in their appearance, he dressed extravagantly, flaunting his wealth before them during a daily procession to the market place, where he would hold court seated on a golden throne. Justice was dispensed in Biblical style, with summary punishments for women who protested at their husbands taking new wives and for young girls who refused to become concubines.

*Jan Bockelson – the man who would be King.*

# THE PEASANTS' APOCALYPSE

**According to Thomas Müntzer (1488-1525), a learned Lutheran minister and would-be messiah, Armageddon was to begin in May 1525. Quite how he arrived at this particular date is unclear, but it seems likely that it was down to pure opportunism on his part, for the German peasants were in revolt at the time and he viewed them as an 'army of light' without a leader.**

Müntzer unfurled his home-made flag in a church in Mühlhausen in April 1523 and using fiery Old Testament rhetoric made an impassioned call to arms. He convinced the ragged but determined rebels that he was the prophet of the apocalypse, sent by the Almighty to lead them in the struggle. Theirs was a just cause. They could not fail. Their oppressors, the nobility and the clergy, were his enemies too, but more than that, they were also the enemies of the Lord.

The truth was rather different. Müntzer secretly harboured an ambition to be the court prophet to the Princes of Saxony, just as Daniel had been at the court of Nebuchadnezzar. If he ingratiated himself with the aristocracy, he thought, he might be able to convince them to aid him in preparing for the Millennium, though quite what this would entail, apart from mass slaughter of the ungodly, is not known. When the princes rejected his advances Müntzer adopted the peasant cause. Each man, he told them, was the source of his own salvation. Each man had the spirit of the living Christ within. Their poverty was the cross upon which they were being martyred, but they need not suffer in silence. He who had faith was righteous, and had no need of the Church and its doctrines. All monks, priests, and godless nobles would be put to the sword. He, Thomas Müntzer, would lead them into battle against these forces of darkness, and, after their inevitable victory, he would help them build the New Jerusalem where all could live in justice and freedom.

But unbeknown to his followers, Müntzer had a blood lust which had been quickened by the disturbing apocalyptic images in the Book of Revelation and the violent deeds described in the Old Testament. He justified his homicidal

actions by convincing himself that society was essentially evil, and that God would not mind if he sent a few sinners to hell ahead of their time. 'The living God is sharpening his scythe in me,' he declared. 'Drive Christ's enemies out from amongst the Elect, for you are the instruments for that purpose ... Don't put up any shallow pretence that God's might will do it without your laying on with the sword ... A godless man has no right to live if he hinders the godly.'

*Müntzer assumed the role of messiah and enlisted the German peasants as his 'army of light'.*

Within a month 8,000 peasants were marshalled under his command, an invincible army of the Lord marching under a white banner emblazoned with a rainbow. However, not everyone saw them as such. A German prince dismissed them as a 'wretched, shabby bag of worms', which provoked Müntzer to retaliate by calling the prince and his peers thieves and murderers. Trading insults was not, however, everyone's idea of the great final battle at the End of Days.

Philip of Hesse, a shrewd young strategist with a sizeable force at his command, was convinced that if he could inflict one serious blow against Müntzer's untrained and undisciplined army, then the entire peasants' revolt would crumble at a stroke. But even that bloody engagement might be avoided if he could persuade the peasants to hand over their 'messiah' in return for a promise to spare their lives.

This was to be Müntzer's biggest test. If his followers doubted his divinity they would not hesitate to hand him over. Faith and human nature had their limits. If he was to win over their eternal souls as well as their hearts and minds Müntzer would have to convince them that their lives were of little consequence in the eternal struggle between good and evil. He covered himself by admitting that there would be a time of darkness and doubt before the new dawn and promised them that the Lord would soon send them a sign to prove that he had made a covenant of peace with the faithful.

**Müntzer promised to catch the enemies' cannonballs in his sleeves.**

At that critical moment, and to Müntzer and everybody else's surprise, a rainbow appeared in the sky - a portent of victory! 'At them, at them!' he urged his startled troops. 'I will catch their cannonballs in my sleeves!' Possessed by the spirit of divine retribution, all 8,000 peasants charged the enemy's lines. They were met by a withering volley from the prince's cannons which broke their courage. In a very short time they disintegrated as an

effective fighting force. The survivors fled in panic, straight into the unsheathed steel of the prince's cavalry. Only a handful of his followers returned home alive. Müntzer escaped, but his prediction, in part at least, would be proved correct. He was caught hiding in a cellar and beheaded on 27 May, the exact month he had predicted as the date of Armageddon.

Incredibly his failure did not deter a series of successors from attempting to establish theoretic dictatorships in Germany and Holland under the Anabaptist banner.

*Müntzer saw himself as both theologian and revolutionary.*

## STORCH — THE MYSTIC AND THE MESSIAH

Thomas Müntzer's vision of the New Jerusalem had been inspired by the radical theories of the German mystic Nicklas Storch. Storch had convinced himself that he had heard the voice of God warning him that the last days were at hand when the righteous, led by the 'elect', would exterminate the ungodly. Storch predicted that this first and last world war would be won by the Turks, after which the Antichrist, roused by the clamour of war and the stench of blood, would assume dominion of the earth.

Storch maintained that only God's elect would then be able to

overthrow the Antichrist and his hordes in a final battle which would see the righteous victorious in time for the Second Coming of Christ and the start of the Millennium.

These apocalyptic predictions, which fired the imaginations of Müntzer and the peasant population, obscured Storch's more interesting ideas, such as the belief that each man contained a spark of the Christ spirit and that he would free this divine part of himself when he turned to God on being 'crucified' by his own personal suffering.

# SABBATAI ZEVI – THE MANIC DEPRESSIVE MESSIAH

**Sabbatai Zevi (1626-76) was the archetypal false prophet. He was learned in the scriptures, charismatic and utterly convincing to those who succumbed to his spell. But his flawed personality also made him extremely dangerous to both the authorities, who feared he would lead a popular uprising, and to his own followers whom he used to feed his megalomania.**

From an early age this withdrawn, spoilt and solitary son of a wealthy Polish merchant, displayed a passion for the Jewish scriptures. His proud father had willingly paid for private religious tuition – until his son's spiritual zeal mutated into an obsession. Although he was a tall, bronzen, bearded, good-looking young man with a 'proud bearing', Sabbatai was crippled by a lack of self-confidence which he compensated for by an affected flamboyance. He suffered from a form of manic depression, which was punctuated by periods of ecstatic bliss. And so it was no surprise when, at the age of sixteen, he swore himself to a rigorous ascetic lifestyle, and withdrew from the world to live the life of a religious recluse. When he re-emerged in 1648, after six long years of prolonged fasting and praying through the night, he had convinced himself that he was the prophet of the new millennium, the saviour of his people.

One evening he calmly strode into the synagogue at Smyrna, his home town, and declared himself to be the Messiah. He might have been dismissed as one of history's many eccentrics had it not been for the fact that large sections of the Jewish community in Poland, and later throughout the world, eagerly accepted him as such.

The Polish Jews were at that time being subjected to another spate of violent pogroms and they were desperate to believe in someone who could spare them further suffering and persecution. The atmosphere of fear and anxiety had given rise to much talk of the Messiah, and Sabbatai certainly cut a convincing figure. But his ecstatic 'fits', which he claimed were symbolic of his people's exile and estrangement from God, failed to convince the rabbinical authorities who considered him no more than an inspired lunatic before banishing him from Smyrna. He may have been the only manic depressive messiah in

*Sabbatai Zevi was incarcerated in the castle of Abydos in Gallipoli, where under pain of death he converted to Islam.*

history, but his timing was impeccable. The year of his appearance on the world stage was 1666, the year to which millennial sects had assigned apocalyptic significance because of the inclusion of the number 666, the number of the Beast in the Book of Revelations. First Palestine and soon the whole world appeared to be talking about Sabbatai, 'the true King Messiah'.

For a time he travelled in Greece where he strode the streets carrying a basket of fish, which he claimed represented the astrological sign of Pisces under which the Jews would be freed from bondage. He was eventually expelled after inviting the Rabbis of Salonika to witness his blasphemous ritual 'marriage' to the Torah, the Book of the Law. Apparently, he was as distressed by his actions as were those who witnessed them and so he sought out a practising Cabbalist, a Jewish mystic, to exorcize his inner 'demons'. But to no avail.

> **Zevi claimed that his 'ecstatic' fits were symbolic of his people's exile and estrangement from God.**

For the next few years he became an itinerant prophet supported by rich devotees who also supplied him with alms which he generously dispensed to the needy. His followers remained convinced of his divinity, despite the fact that his actions were not consistent with those of a model messiah. He was twice married and then swiftly divorced on the grounds that he had not consummated the marriages, because, he claimed, the girls had not been sent from God!

But he swiftly rescinded his rule on celibacy after hearing of a beautiful, promiscuous Polish girl named Sarah, who declared that it was her destiny to be the Bride of the Messiah. He duly sent a delegation to woo her with jewels and fine clothes and a proposal of marriage spiced with pseudo-erotic quotes from the 'Song of Solomon'. Sarah was suitably impressed with his Messianic credentials and the couple were married in Cairo.

By this time some of the faithful were beginning to question their master's motives. Sabbatai's faltering career as a professional prophet was then endorsed by a 22-year-old visionary named Nathan Ashkenazi, whom he had befriended whilst visiting Jerusalem. Nathan dutifully fell into a trance and declared Sabbatai to be the genuine article.

However, not everyone was convinced, and as Sabbatai sailed for Constantinople, his enemies let it be known that Nathan Ashkenazi had predicted that Sabbatai would take the crown from the head of the Sultan of Turkey and place it on his own. Sabbatai's boat was intercepted and he was incarcerated in the castle of Abydos in Gallipoli where he was imprisoned in style, in deference to his Holiness, and allowed visitors. One of these was an equally unstable Jewish mystic who asked Sabbatai to acknowledge him as the Messiah's precursor. When Sabbatai refused, the mystic declared him a fake, whereupon the Sultan gave Sabbatai the choice of death or conversion to Islam. Sabbatai and Sarah chose to convert.

Sabbataism did not, however, die with the man. Those who could not believe that they had been fooled convinced themselves that his conversion was part of the Divine Plan to usurp the enemy from within. Successive generations of believers entrusted their salvation to a series of increasingly radical 'reincarnations' of their leader, such as the eighteenth-century Polish fanatic Jacob Frank, who said that he had been sent to bring about the destruction of the existing world order so that it would be pure for the imminent arrival of God. He encouraged his members to conquer their passions by willingly submitting to temptation, reasoning that only by satiating themselves could they hope to rob sin of its attraction.

## MESSIAH BY NUMBERS

Sabbatai's followers set out to prove that their leader was indeed the long awaited Messiah by the dubious method of mystical word-play known as Gematria. For devout Jews the twenty-two letters of the Hebrew alphabet had occult significance - each letter corresponded to a manifested attribute of God, and so was the 'visible revelation of invisible truth', according to their tradition. In adding up the value of each letter in a name, it was believed that the true identity and destiny of that person would be revealed.

Sabbatai's forename and surname together totalled 814, which, to the delight of his followers, had the same value as that of the most secret name of God. More significantly, it was also the numerical equivalent of the prophetic Hebrew phrase, 'And my year of redemption is come'. But Sabbatai's detractors discovered that 814 also corresponded to the Old Testament phrase, 'And he [Esau] was a cunning hunter, a man of the field', whilst the forename, Sabbatai, had the numerical equivalent of 'Balaam, the Wicked'.

*Sabbatai Zevi imagined himself as the 'true King Messiah', as foretold by Isaiah.*

# THE RANTERS — THE NEW JERUSALEM

**During the Civil War the English nation was divided not only on the question of the King's power over Parliament, but also over religion and the disestablish-** ment of the Church. In this feverish climate millennial hopes were high. A proliferation of self-professed prophets proclaimed the Second Coming of Christ and promised to establish England as the Kingdom of the Saints.

t is extremely unlikely that William Blake drew the inspiration for his poem *Jerusalem* from the activities of the Ranters, those would-be architects of the New Jerusalem who plagued the Puritans in Protector Oliver Cromwell's England. Blake most certainly envisaged something more edifying than the Ranters' idea of Paradise, in which England's green and pleasant land would be overrun with fornicating couples spouting profanities that would make

*Oliver Cromwell forced through the Blasphemy Act of 1650 in a vain attempt to gag the Ranters.*

even a salty sailor blush. The Ranters' central tenet declared that nothing was sinful, for sin was a restraint imposed by a godless society. Moreover, sex, swearing and smoking were to be freely indulged in as a declaration of faith, 'the better to see Christ by', and to show the Ranters' contempt for society.

As a result the Ranters' religious services were radical in the extreme. Their most celebrated 'prophet', Abiezer Coppe, is known to have taken to the pulpit to deliver a torrent of profanities which lasted for a full hour. This habit of spouting spontaneous, uninterrupted doggerel without an obvious point or purpose was a practice of the Ranter prophets from which is derived the modern phrase 'ranting and raving'. During his frequent appearances in the Law Courts, Coppe defended himself by claiming that his rants were prophetic fits brought on by drinking from 'the cup of the Lord's right hand', though it seems highly likely that he was moved by the intoxicating effects of a more secular spirit. His prophetic visions sound suspiciously like the nightmares of an alcoholic, filled as they are with reproach-ful demons and apocalyptic images invoked by an unhealthy obsession with the Book of Revelation.

Even the passing of the Blasphemy Act in 1650 at the insti-gation of Oliver Cromwell failed to gag the Ranters' most outspoken 'prophets'. It was only with the humiliating failure of their two would-be messiahs, John Robbins and Thomas Tany, that the movement disintegrated, the members reluc-tantly deciding to make the best of the England they had.

Although he was hailed as God incarnate, and his wife Joan as the Virgin Mary, John Robbins failed to establish the New Jerusalem at the sect's encampment at Moorfields in the City of London. Perhaps it was the promise of an unvarying diet of raw vegetables, stale bread and water

*Queen Elizabeth I treated false prophets as traitors to the Crown (see box).*

which failed to attract the 144,000 of the 'redeemed' that he required to fulfil the prophecy in the Book of Revelation. Instead Robbins found himself hauled off to prison with only his wife and ten of the faithful to keep him company. There he was given to fits of 'shaking' during which he claimed to receive Divine revelations. This led to him being dubbed the 'Shaker God', although he denied that he was Divine, claiming instead that he was merely 'inspired by the Blessed Spirit'.

## JERUSALEM IN ELTHAM

Robbins' contemporary Thomas Tany fared equally badly. Tany was a goldsmith who was inspired by the voice of God to build the Holy City in the most unprepossessing of places, Eltham in Middlesex. It was a modest and apparently temporary affair, a row of tents each decorated with a sign of one of the twelve tribes of Israel, despite the fact that none of the pioneers was Jewish. Tany, who renamed himself Theaurau John for no particular reason, then got it into his head that he was not only the Saviour of the Jews but also the King of France!

Incredibly, his followers stuck with him and busied themselves erecting defences against the army of the Antichrist which they were sure would soon descend upon them. Instead, Tany grew increasingly impatient and finally declared that the Millennium had been postponed. In a fit of pique he burned his Bible before setting fire to the encampment, consigning the New Jerusalem to the flames. While his followers scrambled to put out the fire, Tany walked off and was never seen again.

> In the Ranters' idea of Paradise, England would be overrun with fornicating couples!

Like Robbins, Tany dismissed scholarship as an intellectual pretension, claiming that he could speak Latin, Hebrew and Greek 'by divine inspiration'. However, his sole contribution to religious literature was a tract entitled *His Auora in Tranlagorum*, written in an unintelligible mixture of pidgin English, schoolboy Latin and even poorer Hebrew. It is a typical example of a Ranter text.

'Doctors, I am the Doctor I am in your method thus a man is, but one man I grant that, but that man of many compounds, you will not deny me this...almo Bonoso almare regel ophronorico ab se sola amantur abo boano so on abscissere.' How his followers could have accepted this gibberish as divinely inspired is anyone's guess, but at least it was free of profanities!

# THE UNHOLY TRINITY

The England of Elizabeth I was a veritable crucible of cults. Most of them were tolerated by the Church authorities, but those who preached 'sedition' were treated as traitors.

The leaders of one of these groups are known only by their surnames: Hacket, Coppinger and Ardington. Hacket, an ill-tempered and illiterate bankrupt who had once bitten off and swallowed the nose of an enemy, believed himself to be Jesus Christ. He boasted of his powers of prophecy and miracle working, which he claimed included the power to bring plague upon England if his demands were not met. Coppinger and Ardington tagged along as his loyal prophets, the former as the 'prophet of mercy' initiating new disciples, and the latter as the 'prophet of

vengeance' responsible for putting the evil eye on dissenters.

The trio were dismissed as 'mere fanatics' until they publicly denounced the Lord Chancellor and the Archbishop of Canterbury as traitors to God and compounded their crime by demanding the abdication of the Queen. They might have got away with a turn or two on the rack had not a few members of the Queen's inner circle been known to agree with them. Her Majesty ordered that the three be tried for treason.

Hacket's final act as he stood on the scaffold was to threaten God Himself with violence if he were not rescued. Coppinger starved himself to death in prison, but Ardington recanted, was released and received a generous pension for his pains.

# JOANNA SOUTHCOTT – MOTHER OF THE MESSIAH

**English eccentric Joanna Southcott (1750-1814) was not content with the fame and huge following that her prophecies brought her. At the advanced age of 65 she announced that, although still a virgin, she was expecting a child. And not just any child; God had apparently chosen Joanna to give birth to the Second Messiah.**

Even as a pious, God-fearing teenager, Joanna's religious experiences had been of biblical proportions. She claimed to have exorcized the Devil from an ailing atheist who had complained that he could hear 'the black dogs of hell' and the 'screams of the damned' outside his sick room window. Feeling 'the pure strength of God' flowing through her veins, Joanna did her Christian duty and commanded the Devil to be gone, whereupon the atheist fell back on his pillow and died.

But it was not until she was in her forties that she began to hear the voice which was to provide her with her prophecies – the voice of God. She nagged bishops, politicians and judges to verify her predictions without success. Eventually she managed to convince a Church of England vicar to accept a sealed envelope which he had to promise not to open until the following Christmas. When he did so he discovered that Joanna had correctly predicted the unexpected death of the Bishop of Exeter, who had been in perfect health at the time she had made the prediction.

In 1801, on the vicar's recommendation, Joanna published the first of many books and pamphlets containing her prophecies. They were often uncannily accurate, but none concerned matters of historical importance, save for one: Joanna predicted the start of the millennium for the year 2014, though on what she based her prediction, no one knows. She refused to divulge her methods to anyone, though it is likely all her prophecies were 'dictated' by her inner voice.

*Cartoonists had a field day at Joanna's expense and lampooned her unmercifully.*

## TICKETS TO PARADISE

These brought her a substantial country-wide following, with 10,000 registered believers at the height of her popularity. Each had to buy a certificate stamped with the Southcottian seal to ensure themselves a place in paradise come the Millennium. Joanna had appropriated the Old Testament myth that only 144,000 of the Elect would be admitted to the Kingdom of God, but was still 134,000 short when it became public knowledge that an infamous murderess had been hanged clutching one of Joanna's sacred certificates!

It is not surprising — given this news, her religious mania and the presence of inner voices — that she was plagued with doubts and given to fits of depression. To set her obviously confused mind at rest she arranged and paid for her own public trial; but with her most devoted disciples, the so-called Southcottians, taking the parts of prosecutor, judge and jury it did not require the talents of a prophet to predict the outcome. Their verdict was that Joanna's visions came 'wholly and entirely from the Spirit of the living Lord'.

## MIRACULOUS CONCEPTION

Even after she had announced that she was 'the second Eve', pregnant with the son of 'the Most High', the faith of her followers did not falter. They showered her with appropriate gifts, including an elaborate and highly expensive satinwood crib. The public at large, however, and in particular the newspapers and satirical cartoonists, lampooned her unmercifully. They took particular pleasure from the announcement that the new Messiah was to be named Shiloh as a result of the Southcottians' misinterpretation of a Biblical prophecy; 'The sceptre shall not depart from Judah, nor a lawgiver from between his feet, until Shiloh come; and unto him shall the gathering of the people be.' *(Genesis, 49:10)*

The fact that Shiloh was not the name of a person, but the name of a town in which the Ark of the Covenant had been kept, did not appear to worry the Southcottians. However, not everyone was amused by Joanna's eccentricities. Effigies of her were burnt in several villages, and in London the main Southcottian chapel was attacked by an angry mob. To defend her claims, Joanna enlisted the services of Dr Reece, an eminent member of the Royal College of Surgeons, who confirmed the pregnancy after an examination during which Joanna had remained fully clothed. She had refused to allow a proper examination, presumably because she felt that it would be unseemly for the mother of the new Messiah to submit to such a demeaning ordeal. She herself was utterly convinced that she was pregnant and her conviction stilled all doubts in her disciples.

However, her own physician, a Dr Mathias, demurred. He diagnosed her condition as 'biliary obstructions' and put her excess weight down to the fact that she spent all day in bed 'in downy indolence'. Undaunted she argued that if she were not pregnant then her symptoms were a sign that something was wrong, something that would soon kill her. Her final prediction proved correct. On 27 December 1814, having grown increasingly frail, Joanna died.

On her written instructions, Reece and Mathias conducted a post-mortem in her cramped and dingy apartment in the presence of thirteen medical experts and a group of her closest followers. The doctors' report was a grave disappointment to her disciples. Reece concluded that she had been suffering from what we would now call a phantom pregnancy brought on by her religious obsession. 'Neither the promised Shiloh nor any other foetus was found within.'

## SECRETS OF THE SEALED BOX

Prior to her death Joanna Southcott had prepared a sealed box supposedly containing the secret of world peace and her predictions for the following centuries. She left special instructions that the box was only to be opened in a time of national crisis and then only in the presence of 24 bishops of the Church of England!

In 1927 the box was sent to the National Laboratory of Psychical Research, where researcher Harry Price x-rayed it only to discover a horse pistol, a dice box, a purse, several books, a lottery ticket and a night cap. Undeterred, the English Panacea Society, formed to promote her writings, continues to maintain that they hold the 'real' Southcott box, and that 'crime and banditry, distress of nations and perplexity will continue to increase until the bishops open Joanna Southcott's box of sealed writings'.

*Joanna's sealed box promised further predictions for the following centuries, but in fact it contained only trinkets.*

> An infamous killer had been hanged clutching one of Joanna's certificates.

# MILLER'S MISCALCULATION

**In May 1832 the people of the eastern states of America were thrown into an escalating wave of panic by the predictions of the Endtime prophet William Miller. Miller, a wealthy farmer and a Baptist preacher, had been obsessed with uncovering the date ordained by the Divine for the Second Coming and the beginning of the Millennium, a date which he believed was encrypted in the Bible.**

After months of complex calculations, derived from figures in the Book of Daniel, Miller finally announced that the end of the world was at hand; it would come in 1843. 'The evidence flows in from every quarter,' he declared with confidence. Within a short time he had attracted a 50,000-strong following drawn from many denominations, each impressed by his modest demeanour and apparent sincerity. They took the name Millerites and declared that they were commanded 'to occupy ourselves until Christ comes. We are to do good as we have the opportunity, and by no means spend our time in idleness.'

While the Millerites prepared themselves with prayer and pious deeds, the public panicked. People went about with an umbrella in the belief that when the time came it would help them ascend to heaven. One wealthy woman even

*The Great Day as prophesied by the Adventists.*

went so far as to strap herself to a trunk brimming with valuables in the hope that when she was taken heavenwards the trunk would be taken up with her!

Others gave away their possessions, so certain were they of their own impending death, and were later shocked to be told they could not have them back. Everywhere shops and businesses closed down. One notice read: 'This shop is closed in honour of the King of Kings who will appear about the 20th October.'

America was gripped by Endtime fever. Prominent men of religion and letters were asked for their expert opinions by newspaper men desperate to keep the story on the front pages. The philosopher Ralph Waldo Emerson was reported to have dismissed the prediction with the comment: 'It doesn't much concern me. I live in Boston.'

Miller had originally given April 1843 as the day of Christ's descent, but the month passed without the King of Kings putting in an appearance. May, June and July duly went by, all without a portent of doom or even a sign in the sky. Bewildered but unshaken, Miller revised his calculations to take account of discrepancies between the Christian and Jewish calendars. This resulted in a postponement of the apocalypse until March 1844. The Millerites were heartened, sales of umbrellas soared and the wealthy woman patiently continued her vigil still strapped to her trunk of valuables.

**America was gripped by Endtime fever.**

March 1844 also proved to be an uneventful month. One of Miller's inner circle suggested that perhaps the Messiah might prefer to appear instead on the Jewish day of Atonement, 22 October, and the new date was duly proclaimed. When October came and went without incident the world damned the Millerites and went about its business as before. The date is still referred to as 'the Great Disappointment' by Seventh-Day Adventists, the sect which succeeded the Millerites.

Disheartened and in failing health, Miller admitted that he had been a fool to pride and fanaticism and blamed his enthusiasm on the wave of hysteria in which he, too, had been caught up. Shortly before his death in 1849 he declared, 'I do not wonder that the world calls us insane; for I confess it looks like insanity to me to see religious, candid men spend their time and talents on questions of so little consequence to us here or hereafter.'

His remaining handful of followers were undeterred. They comforted themselves with the thought that the Second Coming may well have occurred, but on the plane of spirit rather than in the world of matter.

*William Miller: he later admitted to being a fool to pride and fanaticism, but his followers continue to live in hope.*

## FLAWED ARITHMETIC

Miller's calculations derived from his interpretation of the Book of Daniel. He assumed that a reference to one day in the Bible meant one year of earthly time; therefore, when the biblical prophet spoke of seventy weeks as being the time until the anointment of 'the most Holy', Miller took it to mean 490 years. When this was added to 457 BC, the date Ezra, the Jewish priest, was permitted by the Persian king Artaxerxes to return to Jerusalem to reconstitute observance of Jewish law and worship, it gave the year 33 AD, the year of the crucifixion. In Miller's mind this seemed to confirm his theory and spurred him on. He next examined a passage which held 2300 days as the time needed to purify the sanctuary, which he took to mean the cleansing of the earth for the return of Christ. This seemed to him to be confirmed when Daniel asks for the meaning of the phrase and is told 'at the time of the end shall be the vision'.

It was by adding 2,300 years to 457 BC that Miller arrived at the fateful year 1843. He could still be right, if the 2300 'days' were to run from the crucifixion and not 457 BC, as he assumed. If that is the case, we will have to wait until 2333 AD to find out!

# THE MORMONS

**The Mormons are unique among the world's major religious sects in that they believe the year 2000 marks both the secular and spiritual Millennium. Theirs is an unquestioning faith, based on a literal interpretation of the Gospels and the angelic teachings entrusted to their own 'prophet' Joseph Smith, who insisted that the unrepentant must convert before the Second Coming, or face eternal damnation.**

M embers of the Church of Jesus Christ of Latter-Day Saints, or Mormons as they are more commonly known, put their faith in a singularly American form of millennarianism. They believe that Jesus Christ entrusted their 'prophet' with 'the truth' and that the New Jerusalem will be established in America.

The religion was founded in extraordinary circumstances. Fourteen-year-old Joseph Smith, the son of immigrant parents, claimed to have been praying in the woods near his home in Vermont, New England, one day in 1820 when he encountered two angels. 'This is my beloved Son, hear Him!' said one of the other. Assuming one to be God and

*A Mormon temple in Maryland, USA, surrounded by Christmas lights.*

the other Christ, Smith asked them which church he should join in order to be saved. When the first angel answered that all creeds were 'an abomination', Smith decided to form his own.

He claimed to have received further encouragement two years later, when a second visitation brought an angel who urged him to spread the Gospel. To aid him in his mission the angel, whom Smith called Mormon, revealed the location of a hidden book said to record the 'fullness of the everlasting Gospel' as told to the original inhabitants of North America by Jesus Christ. The text had been preserved on plates of gold which Smith was to translate, but not until he had proven himself worthy by visiting the site annually for the next four years. Only then would he be allowed to take them home.

Sceptical non-believers might explain the delay by suggesting that this was the time Smith needed to write the text himself, a suspicion which must have troubled his potential patron and publisher, Martin Harris, who was apparently not content to finance publication until he had satisfied himself as to its authenticity.

## ANGELIC TEXT

Harris submitted the transcript, which consisted of a concoction of ancient languages with an accompanying translation, to a noted academic, Professor Charles Anthon. Anthon is said to have declared it to be a jumble of 'Egyptian, Chaldean, Assyriac and Arabic' characters, which nevertheless appeared to make sense and was considered too complex to have been faked by someone of Smith's limited education. That settled, it was duly published in March 1830 under the title *The Book of Mormon*. The Mormon Church was constituted just days later.

> Those who have been baptized will fly up to meet the Messiah.

Smith's standing as a genuine prophet has been further undermined, in the opinion of non-believers, by the fact that he claimed that the spirit of John the Baptist later initiated him into 'the priesthood of Aaron', a line of High Priests who were exclusively Jewish. However, if the 'Book of Mormon' were not a complete fabrication, then it might have been what in modern parlance would be called a 'channelled' teaching, with Smith as the medium for a higher intelligence, perhaps even his own. However, from the pedantic nature of the prophecies it would appear that even if that were so, this particular medium limited the value of the message by insisting on the literal truth of the Bible.

*Smith built his following by preaching in the wilderness.*

## THE MORMON PROPHECIES

One of the conditions of the Second Coming, according to the Mormons, is that the ten tribes of Israel must gather in Israel and America en masse. The tribe of Ephraim are to congregate at the site of the New Jerusalem, near the Rocky Mountains, while the descendants of the Kingdom of Judah must rebuild the Temple in Jerusalem to fulfil the Old Testament prophecy. With the prospect of a permanent Israeli-PLO peace treaty this prophecy might yet become a reality before the turn of the century. However, the most problematic part will be identifying those who belong to the ten lost tribes of Israel. Even in the extremely unlikely event that they are tracked down, they will have to be persuaded to travel to America to witness the Second Coming of a man they rejected as their Messiah the first time round.

Assuming that this miracle does occur in 2000, we are then to expect the materialization of the City of Enoch (the New Jerusalem) in the Rockies, followed by the resurrection of those who have been baptized into the Mormon faith, who will rise from their graves and fly up to meet the Messiah. The good news is that you do not have to be a Mormon to be in on this - the 'good heathen' also qualifies. The wicked, however, will be cast down into a subterranean realm for the entire thousand years of Christ's reign.

During the thousand year-idyll of the Mormon Millennium, Satan will be chained; those who are unrepentant will die, while those who embrace the faith will be made immortal. Although Satan will be freed in 3000AD, he and his army will be defeated and the world will be 'celestialized' for the immortals.

*Joseph Smith – was he a fake or an inspired medium?*

# 'THE HOUSE OF HORROR'

**The graphic and gory scenes in the film** *The Exorcist* **pale in comparison to the bloody events that took place during Easter 1823 in a pretty family house in Switzerland. One of history's few female would-be messiahs, Margaret Peter could not wait for the army of the Lord, so she initiated her own Armageddon.**

The Peter house, in the village of Wildisbuch, was the family home of widower Johannes Peter, his son and five daughters. Born in 1793, Margaret was the youngest and her father's favourite. Pampered and precocious, she dominated her elder siblings, exerting a strange hold over the entire household that was to have tragic consequences for them all. In her youth, Margaret exhibited a religious mania which drove her to preach hell and damnation, both in public and before her adoring family, who looked at her in reverential wonder, unquestioningly accepting her words as the Will of God.

Her congregation swiftly grew as her reputation as a Bible-thumping revivalist spread throughout the region. By March 1823, the Peter house was home to a number of her most devoted disciples, whose loyalty was soon to be tested to the limit.

Margaret spent most of that month locked in her room, reading the Bible and praying for guidance. When she emerged, just before Easter, she declared that Armageddon was nigh and that the site of the final battle was to be the Peter house. Satan had apparently taken refuge in a nest in the roof, but Margaret was empowered to evict him. After a week of prayer and rituals, which included the violent exorcizing of minor demons from various members of the household, Margaret led a small party upstairs, armed with axes, hammers and clubs. While she sat on the bed directing their assault on the invisible enemy, her disciples made a frenzied attack on the furniture, reducing everything to kindling and demolishing a wall in the process.

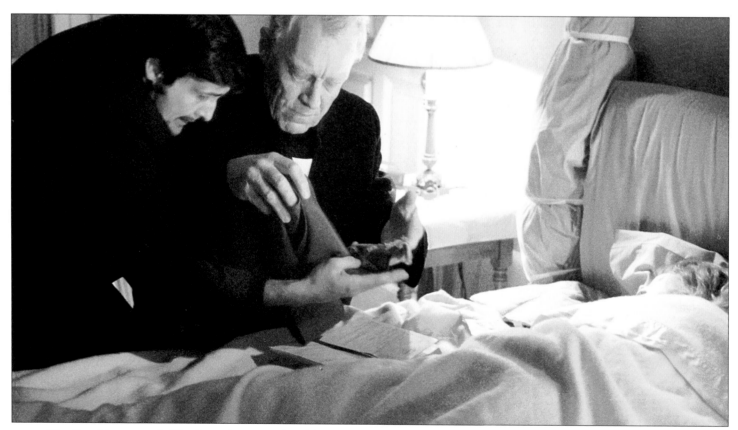

*The disturbing scenes in* The Exorcist *were eclipsed by the real-life exorcism perpetrated by 'holy' Margaret.*

## BLOOD SACRIFICE

The neighbours looked on through the gaping hole with a mixture of amusement and horror until the authorities arrived, to be damned as the army of the Antichrist by the messiah herself. The family were arrested, but released pending a doctor's report, a report which would, had it come in time, have committed Margaret and her sister Elisabeth to an asylum.

A few days later, they all returned to the house where Margaret took her twelve-strong 'congregation' to an upper room and there accused her brother Caspar of being possessed by the devil. He was so mesmerized by his sister that he stood unresisting while she beat the devil out of him with a wedge. As he was led downstairs, his clothes matted with blood, Margaret prepared the final act in her perverted Passion play. 'I shall offer myself up as the final sacrifice,' she announced, 'so that Satan may be defeated.'

Elisabeth sought to upstage her, begging to be sacrificed instead, and, to prove her eagerness, hit herself on the head with a mallet. 'It has been revealed to me that

*Dusted with ashes, covered with garlands of flowers, his tongue pierced by an iron spike, a young Indian is taken to a temple for exorcism. Margaret Peter's methods were even more violent and extreme.*

## BACK FROM THE DEAD

To outsiders it seems incredible that so many would-be messiahs are able to keep the unquestioning faith of their followers without having to demonstrate their powers or prove their 'divinity'. In time, however, all must face the ultimate test: their resurrection from the dead.

Towards the end of the eighteenth century, a young American Quaker woman, Jemima Wilkinson, overcame that problem by first rising from the dead and then forming a sect.

Jemima appeared to have suffered a natural death and was declared stone cold dead when she was nailed up in her coffin. On the way to the graveyard, she came to life and thereupon declared that this was a sign that God had chosen her to build a new church in preparation for Christ's return in 1786.

Her sect was strictly celibate and dedicated to good works, particularly among the native Americans, earning Jemima the title 'The Universal Friend'. Perhaps this is why her followers were willing to forgive her when Christ failed to appear at the appointed date.

Nevertheless, she must have sensed their disappointment, for she then claimed to be able to walk on water, and offered to prove it. However, when her followers affirmed their belief in her she was satisfied to let it go at that.

Her followers may have been temporarily appeased, but when she failed to return as promised following her second 'death', in 1820, they were disillusioned and the sect was disbanded. While Jemima may have been genuinely deluded, many modern messiahs have cynically used this 'doubt-me-and-I'll-kill-myself' brinkmanship to control their believers. One wonders what a psychiatrist would make of leaders like these who use the tactics of an attention-seeking toddler!

Elisabeth shall sacrifice herself,' cried Margaret setting about her sister with a hammer. The others in the group joined in, urged on by Margaret's screams of 'Die for Christ, Elisabeth!'

Still Satan was not beaten. Margaret commanded the others to make a cross from the loosened floorboards before giving her final order. 'You must crucify me,' she said. At first they refused, but Margaret promised them that as the true messiah she would rise again in three days and usher in the true Millennium. Those who held back she threatened. 'You will be responsible for all the souls that will be lost unless you fulfil what I have appointed you to do.' And she assured them that a final, bloody act would be rewarded by a thousand years of peace for all humanity.

**After the bloodbath the murderers calmly ate their lunch.**

Margaret made no protest as the nails were driven into her. Her mania had made her impervious to pain. 'Now finish the task,' she shrieked at them. 'Drive a nail through my heart.' One of the women stabbed her instead with a knife, but it did not kill her. 'Beat in my skull,' demanded their mad messiah, and they duly obliged. The disciples then calmly went downstairs and ate their lunch.

For the next three days they faithfully watched over the corpses, eagerly anticipating 'holy' Margaret's resurrection. When she failed to appear, the deaths were reported and in time the disciples were put on trial. As they began their prison sentences the house was levelled to the ground; then the authorities ordered that nothing was ever again to be erected on the site.

# THE PRINCE OF PROPHETS

In nineteenth-century Victorian England, sex and sin were virtually synonymous, such was the prudish character of that society. It was an age when even piano legs would be covered to avoid offending the sensibilities of polite society and ladies were expected to endure, rather than enjoy, the sexual act. Only the 'godless' lower classes were thought to take any pleasure from gratifying their desires, while everyone else was expected to feel guilty.

The Reverend Henry James Prince, a self-proclaimed prophet, exploited the prevailing attitude by founding a sect which professed to be a sanctuary of spiritual love, but was little more than an elaborate front to enable him to satisfy his secular appetites. Prince, a former Church of England preacher, had been expelled from the Church amid rumours that he had forced his un-Christian attentions on the female members of his flock. Undaunted, he set up his own chapel in the English seaside town of Brighton, then a very fashionable resort, and within a short time had a sizeable congregation drawn from the moneyed middle classes.

Almost all of Prince's devotees were insular, unfulfilled young women who lacked a sense of purpose in their lives. He provided them with an opportunity to channel their repressed energies into a spiritual cause he called 'The Abode of Love', one of the first religious communes in England. To escape prying eyes he relocated to a 200-acre sanctuary near Spaxton in Somerset, with a manor house, stables, cottages and a private chapel that would serve as the headquarters of his sect, the Agapemonites. The name was derived from the Greek term for spiritual love, and was intended to recall the *agapae*, or love feasts, celebrated by the early Christians.

## IMMORTAL AND PERFECT

Mesmerized by this slim, soft-spoken man with a beguiling smile, the daughters of suburban socialites left their homes and followed him to Spaxton. The estate had been bought and lavishly refurbished with the generous donations of these disciples, many of whom had sold their property and cashed in their savings. Prince renamed himself the 'Beloved One', the prophet of the new paradise, and indoctrinated his female admirers in his peculiar philosophy in preparation for the coming millennium. 'The human body dwells in an enemy's country, amidst enemies,' he told them, 'all of whom are in league with that enemy within him – death.' He, Henry Prince, was unafraid of death for he was immortal and could offer immortality to those who would follow him. He was the Prince of Prophets, the natural successor to Adam, Noah, Abraham and Jesus, a perfect man, impervious to sin. 'I am one in the flesh with Christ. I died and was renewed in the Spirit to do his work.' According to Prince, this work involved

*To ensure privacy Prince established a private commune on a 200-acre estate in Somerset.*

taking a spiritual marriage partner, but refraining from consummating the union until the Second Coming. Whenever the urge to sin proved too strong to be subdued by reading the scriptures, both gentlemen and ladies were encouraged to play billiards until the desire wore off.

Prince claimed to be above such temptation himself, but once he had satisfied himself that his orders would be obeyed without question the time came for him to 'sacrifice' his perfection to 'complete the great work of reconciling the fallen creature to the Holy One.' He declared that, 'It was God's purpose to extend His love from heaven to earth, from spirit to flesh, from soul to body. Jesus Christ was going to carry out his purpose of grace and love towards the flesh, to save it, not by telling or explaining to flesh what his mind was towards it, but by living it out, through his own spirit'. In short, they would not wait for the Messiah. The prophet would take a partner, a young virgin to be known as the 'Bride of the Lamb'. With the consummation of their marriage, the community would be purged of all sin and the disciples would be miraculously freed from the flesh to live eternally in the world of spirit. Then, and only then would the Millennium begin.

**When the urge for sex proved too strong, they played billiards.**

Prince announced that he would accept whichever partner God chose for him, but unknown to the eager, expectant women he had already made his choice. It was to be Zoe Paterson, the prettiest and youngest of the disciples. However, to the great disappointment of the community, the blessed union did not herald the promised Millennium, an age Prince had cynically described as the 'Great Manifestation of God's Love'. Despite increasing disquiet, Prince, having secured his young mistress in marriage, would not give her up and the sect began to break up amid accusations that Miss Paterson was not the first disciple their 'perfect' prophet had seduced.

The 'Bride of the Lamb' eventually became the mother of a baby girl, but the child was disowned by her 'perfect' parents as 'Satan's offspring', as were the other babies who were born over the years.

*Prince enjoyed the fruits of the new paradise he created.*

# BE FRUITFUL AND MULTIPLY

For Claus Ludwig, the sixteenth-century German Anabaptist and self-made messiah, sex was the only true sacrament. Ludwig preached that man was bread and woman was wine. Only when joined in sexual union were they in holy communion. He set about recruiting the army of Armageddon, 144,000 righteous souls to annihilate the wicked, but most of his congregation preferred to celebrate their version of Holy Communion than save a sinner.

Members were known as Bloodfriends and had the power to liberate and purify others through copulation. Bloodfriends who became pregnant were promised that they would be free from the pain of childbirth and their offspring would be holy. Ludwig was destined to be the father of the one who would be known as the 'Judge of the World'. To this end, all the female members were required to sleep with him. Bloodfriend services always ended with the command, 'Be fruitful and multiply', which signalled the beginning of the ritual orgy, but full members did not have to wait for the sanction of the service. As all desires were said to be prompted by the Holy Ghost, members were encouraged to give vent to them whenever they pleased. Despite the sect's efforts to appear respectable by attending orthodox church services, their activities were uncovered. In 1551 three members were executed, the remainder recanted and Ludwig fled, never to be heard of again.

# MADAME BLAVATSKY

**With only a few years of the twentieth century remaining, it is unlikely that the outlandish predictions of Madame Blavatsky, the eccentric Victorian psychic and co-founder of the Theosophist Society, will be fulfilled. Nevertheless, her dramatic prophecies and fanciful theories remain an influence on many modern seers and esoteric societies.**

Helena Petrovna Blavatsky (1831-91) was one of the most flamboyant figures to grace the Victorian era. She was born into the Russian aristocracy, but was said to swear like a sailor and to be in the habit of soothing her nerves by taking marijuana. An insatiable passion for travel and adventure took her, at the age of sixteen, first to America, where she claimed to have

*Krishnamurti with Annie Besant (Blavatsky's successor). He rejected the role of messiah.*

witnessed voodoo ceremonies in New Orleans, and then to Tibet, where she immersed herself in the Eastern esoteric tradition. On her return to Russia she found herself in the spiritualist firmament.

Occultism and anything connected with the exotic East or Egypt was then in fashion and so Blavatsky was courted by high society, who delighted in her demonstrations of psychic phenomena. Her first book, *Isis Unveiled*, was soon a topic of fashionable conversation, though today her dubious theories are seen as a hotch-potch of Eastern mysticism and Western mythology, rooted in the erroneous belief that the 'lost' continents of Atlantis and Lemuria had once been the centres of civilization.

## THE SECRET MASTERS

She claimed this book contained the 'master-key to the mysteries of ancient and modern science and theology' and had been dictated to her by spirit guides, whom she called the Secret Masters. Her claims were given some credence by her friend, the co-founder of the Theosophical Society, Colonel H S Olcott, a rather serious-minded man who had fought in the American Civil War. He regularly observed her in a trance-like state, 'pen flying over the page ... she would suddenly stop, look into space with the vacant eye of the clairvoyant seer, shorten her vision so as to look at something held invisibly in the air before her, and begin copying on the paper what she saw. The quotation finished, her eyes would resume their natural expression.'

Madame Blavatsky was not content with being a celebrated psychic, however. She petitioned her spirit guides to help make her the seer of the century. In her second book, *The Secret Doctrine*, she detailed her vision of the occult evolution of the cosmos, culminating with a description of the world to come. According to her Secret Masters, we are the fifth of six races of man predestined to walk the earth, and we can expect the emergence of the next race within our lifetimes. 'Occult philosophy teaches that even now, under our very eyes, the new Race and Races are preparing to be formed, and that it is in America that the transformation will take place, and has already silently commenced.'

The USA, she claimed, was the seed bed of the 'primary race', where the 'germs of the Sixth sub-race' will develop. Drawing on the Hindu theory of the Manvantara, Blavatsky predicted that 25,000 years after this the 'New Americans' will give birth to the seventh sub-race, 'until, in consequence of cataclysms, the first series of those which must one day destroy Europe, and still later the whole Aryan race (and thus affect both Americas), as also most of the lands directly connected with the confines of our continent and isles – the Sixth Root-Race will have appeared'

This phase of evolution will initially manifest itself in human beings who will be regarded as 'abnormal oddities physically and mentally'. She then predicted the dramatic appearance of a new continent arising out of the sea, where the

*Madame Blavatsky - eccentric Victorian psychic, prophetess and founder of the Theosophical Society*

new Sixth Race will settle, ensuring its survival from the global cataclysm to come. When this 'general disaster' will befall us, Blavatsky could not say, but she did foresee that 'the final cataclysm will be preceded by many smaller submersions and destructions both by wave and volcanic fires.' Mankind might even transcend the body and exist in the spirit, if we can raise our psychic vibrations to the right level! Whether or not we achieve this refined level of consciousness, Blavatsky assures us that following the cataclysms, our descendants will witness a Golden Age, for a 'grander and far more glorious Race than any of those we know of at present', though she predicted that the Seventh Race will begin the next phase of evolution on the planet Mercury!

> **The Seventh Race will begin the next phase of evolution on the planet Mercury.**

Blavatsky promised that psychic powers and esoteric knowledge – the secrets of the spheres – would be the 'inheritance of these future Races'. However, if her final prophecy, concerning the worldwide acceptance of her own esoteric philosophy, is indicative of her accuracy, we are still a long way from extinction. 'The truths of today are the falsehoods and errors of yesterday and vice versa. It is only in the 20th century that portions, if not the whole, of the present work will be vindicated.'

## THE COMING OF MAITREYA

Madame Blavatsky adopted many Buddhist concepts into the doctrines of the Theosophical Society, amongst which was the belief in the coming of Maitreya, a world teacher. In Buddhist philosophy a Buddha, or Enlightened One, appears at significant moments in history to renew the teachings of Gautama, the founder of Buddhism. According to tradition, the next Buddha will be known as Maitreya (the kind one), whom Blavatsky predicted would be born in 1950. 'We are at the close of the cycle of five thousand years of the present Aryan Kali Yuga, or Dark Age,' she wrote. 'This will be succeeded by an age of light ... A new messenger of the spirit will be sent to the western nations.'

Unfortunately for the Theosophists, Blavatsky's successors, Annie Besant and C W Leadbeater, could not wait until 1950. In 1910 they travelled to India, where they found the 15-year-old Jiddu Krishnamurti playing on a beach. They declared him to be a new messiah, the reincarnation of Krishna and Jesus Christ. Besant and Leadbeater adopted the boy and groomed him for his new role. However, in 1929, to their embarrassment, he rejected their patronage and their philosophy, declaring: 'You can form other organizations and expect someone else. With that I am not concerned, nor with creating new cages ... My only concern is to set men absolutely, unconditionally free.'

Ironically, after he had rejected all religions as 'refuges' and refused to accept the role of Messiah, Krishnamurti went on to become one of the great spiritual leaders of the twentieth century. He was a world teacher in practice if not in name.

*The Theosophical Society is still active in over 60 countries.*

# ALEISTER CROWLEY —
# THE DARK GURU

**The notorious magician Aleister Crowley (1875-1947) adopted the title of 'The Great Beast 666' from the *Book of Revelation* and proclaimed himself prophet of a new age. It was to be the 'Aeon of Horus', presided over by the hawk-headed Egyptian god of war, for which Crowley correctly predicted the outbreak of the two World Wars and forecast another major eastern European conflict for 1997.**

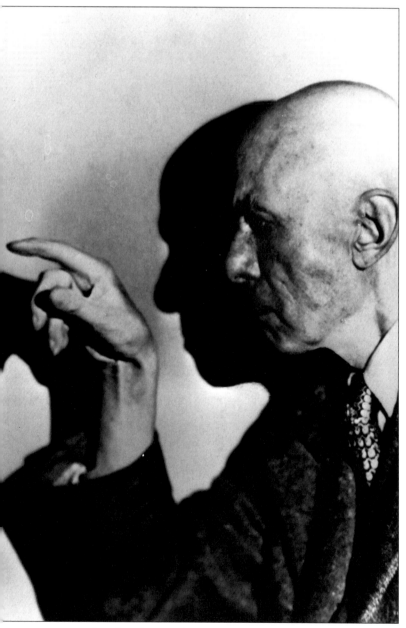

*Crowley photographed two years before he died alone, penniless and apparently 'perplexed'.*

E dward Alexander Crowley, the son of strict parents, who combined membership of the puritanical Plymouth Brethren with the ownership of a brewery, saw himself as the dark guru of a new pagan religion opposed to the Edwardian establishment in general and Christianity in particular. His favourite dictum, borrowed from Blake and Rabelais, was 'Do what thou wilt shall be the whole of the law', which was wilfully misinterpreted by hippies and hedonists in the 1960s and

**The press dubbed him 'The Wickedest Man In The World'.**

now by those who wish to perpetuate the Crowley myth. But far from being the guru of an alternative society, Crowley was self-centred and conceited; he despised anyone who slavishly followed him, particularly the neurotic women who became his disciples, and took an adolescent delight in shocking Edwardian society and mocking its conventions. This prompted the English press to call him 'the wickedest man in the world', although he has been more accurately described as 'a nasty little boy who never grew up'.

A precociously gifted student, he graduated from Cambridge at the age of 23 and joined the Order of the Golden Dawn, a fashionable occult society which included the poet W B Yeats among its more illustrious members. But Crowley's relationship with the Order was short-lived and acrimonious. He made himself generally disagreeable and fell out with the founder who died, it is claimed, after losing a 'magical battle' to 'the Great Beast' on the astral plane.

## A NEW AEON

Retreating to Egypt in 1904 with his clairvoyant wife Rose, Crowley claimed to have made contact with a spirit guide called Aiwass who used Rose as a medium to dictate the text of what became 'The Book of the Law', a magical text heralding the end of the age of Osiris, the 'dying god' and the beginning of the age of Horus.

By 1910 Crowley had indulged himself to excess. He was addicted to morphine and preaching was not a new religion, but a very old one which he called 'Sexmagick'. He established a Temple in London and another in the more agreeable surroundings of Cefalu in Sicily, which he called the Abbey of Thelema (borrowing the name from Rabelais). After three years of drugs and debauchery the Italian government finally expelled him, the last straw being the mysterious death of a disciple who had allegedly drunk cat's blood during a ritual. Crowley returned to England where he faded into obscurity, spending his last days penniless and apparently frightened of the dark in a gloomy boarding house in the Sussex seaside town of Hastings. His last words were, 'I am perplexed.'

**Crowley claimed that belief in his prophecies could bring them into being.**

Crowley claimed that the The Book of the Law did not simply record his prophecies, but could bring them into being through the will and imagination of those who read and believed in them. He understood that the power of thought is the most potent force in creation and lies at the heart of ceremonial magic. To believe that something will happen is sometimes enough to make it happen. Perhaps if the cult which has grown up around Aleister Crowley, and our fascination with the dark side of human nature, eventually loses its appeal the new age he envisaged will be considerably brighter. His prophecies were no doubt made for the sake of sensation, but he knew that will power is the most potent force we possess for determining our own future.

*Did Crowley correctly predict the Civil War in Yugoslavia or the conflict in Chechnya.*

# PROPHET OF THE APOCALYPSE

In addition to encouraging everyone to lose their inhibitions and indulge themselves without fear of guilt - 'Take your fill and will of love as ye will, when, where and with whom ye will' - *The Book of the Law* described the world as it would be during the coming age. Horus would ascend his throne during a period of violence, widespread destruction and fire which, judging by clues in the text, could well have been the beginning of thetwentieth century. In the third chapter is the prophetic line, 'I am the warrior Lord of the Forties', which seems to be a clear reference to World War II – all this in a book published in 1904.

Of more immediate interest are the many veiled references to European wars in 1997, which Crowley predicted would ravage the Balkans and former Soviet states. However the encoded prophecies are too vague to tell if he was predicting the resumption of

fighting in the former Yugoslavia and the continuance of the war in Chechnya or the outbreak of new conflicts.

Whichever it is it will culminate in the appearance of another Egyptian warrior god, Ra-Hoor-Khuit, who will judge humanity, regenerate the Earth and herald the next Aeon, a golden age strangely reminiscent of the psychedelic 1960s.

'Another prophet shall arise, and bring fresh fever from the skies ... Invoke me under my stars! Love is the law, Love under Will ... take wine and strange drugs ... and be drunk thereof. They shall not harm ye at all.' Is it possible that Crowley actually foresaw the Hippie culture which flowered in the 1960s, or was it simply wishful thinking on his part to imagine an age of free love and free drugs at a time when preaching such things had led to him being labelled as the avatar of wickedness?

# THE BLACK MESSIAHS

**The Christian missionaries in Africa believed that they were bringing the light of the Lord to the Dark continent, spreading a gospel of hope which promised the natives freedom from the slavery of their heathen gods. In many cases, however, the Biblical prophecies served only to strengthen the people's burning desire to be free of their white colonial masters and to reinforce the conviction that they were right to demand it.**

I n the 1920s Simon Kimbangu was working as a servant in a white household, until, fired by Bible readings from the British Baptist Mission, he began to have visions of God. The visions apparently blessed him with prophetic powers and the ability to heal the sick. Some said he was even able to revive the dead. The white authorities tolerated Kimbangu's activities so long as he continued to preach in favour of monogamy and against idolatry. But when he began to prophesy that the whites would one day be forced to pack their bags and flee, they imprisoned him. He died in jail in 1950, but long after his death his followers persisted in their belief that Kimbangu, 'the Black Prophet', continued to live amongst them in spirit.

*The Native Americans had no concept of an apocalyptic battle between Good and Evil until it was introduced to them by Christian missionaries.*

John Masowe, 'God's Messenger', came to South Africa from Rhodesia with his followers in the 1940s. In his former homeland he had been inspired by visions of the apocalypse which had been described to him by missionaries from the American Watch Tower movement. The Watch Tower Movement insisted that the Second Coming of Christ had already occurred, but that the Messiah was invisible. The Day of Judgement, they said, had arrived. But for Masowe the Millennium would not begin until the whites were driven from Africa. And that included their missionaries!

**The Watch Tower Movement insisted that the Second Coming of Christ had already occurred, but that the Messiah was invisible.**

Masowe and other African messiahs had no fear of the Day of Wrath, which they felt was to be the day of their deliverance from white oppression. Had not the missionaries explained that this would be the day God would punish the sinful? And was the white man not guilty of the most grievous sins for enslaving his black brothers?

Although Masowe assured his followers that they were immortal, he refused to lead them into an armed struggle against the whites. Instead he staked his claim to a region he believed would one day be their Promised Land and built his church there. To protect himself and his inner circle, he assumed a number of false names and registered the church in the South African Companies' Register as a furniture factory. To this day his whereabouts remain unknown.

Not all of the African people embraced the Christian gospels. Enoch Mgijima, 'bishop, prophet and guardian' of Queenstown, South Africa, denounced the New Testament as white propaganda. Instead he took his creed from the Old Testament and convinced his 500 followers that they were the true Israelites, Jehovah's Chosen People. Accordingly they celebrated the Jewish festivals, the Sabbath and the high holy days amidst the poverty of the townships where they lived and waited patiently to be led by their messiah into the Promised Land of a new South Africa.

The government was not so patient and demanded that the sect disband. Mgijima responded by inciting his people to defend their faith with the few weapons they had at their disposal, sticks and spears. During the ensuing battle one hundred of his followers were killed and the sect was dispersed.

Ironically, South Africa would be freed from minority rule 50 years later, but not by a messiah in the spiritual sense of the word, and not, fortunately, through violence.

# NATIVE AMERICANS

The Native American Indians had no need to believe in a saviour or messiah until the white man made them second-class citizens in their own country. With the buffalo slaughtered and their people corralled in reservations the Indians of the nineteenth century looked to men like Handsome Lake, Smohalla and John Wovoka to predict the Day of Judgement when the whites would be swallowed up by the earth.

Handsome Lake (born 1775) was a visionary who claimed to have been entrusted with a sacred mission to save the tribes from the addictive demon, alcohol. Influenced by the Quakers, he preached abstinence, fidelity and a return to the traditional values of his ancestors.

Whilst some of the Native American messiahs preached violence against the oppressors, Smohalla argued for passive resistance. Described as an 'odd little wizard of an Indian', given to visionary fits, Smohalla predicted that the time would come when their saviour would appear to turn the white man from their land. In the meantime they were to resist all efforts that were being made to turn them into farmers, because by ploughing the land they were harming the sacred Mother Earth.

'Men who work cannot dream,' he would say, 'and wisdom comes to us in dreams.'

The Paviotsos prophet Wodziwob predicted that the sins of the white man would be repaid when the earth opened up and swallowed them all, leaving their property for the Indians. He taught his followers the Ghost Dance, which symbolized this event and which is still performed on reservations in the Northwest.

His successor, John Wovoka, helped establish the Ghost Dance religion after being convinced that he had heard the voice of the Great Spirit. Wovoka predicted that the Day of Judgement would see the white man carried off by a cyclone, the return of the buffalo and with them, the dignity of the Indian nation.

*The Christian missionaries regarded the settlements as outposts in a war against the ungodly.*

# SAVAGE MESSIAH – CHARLES MANSON

**On 9 August 1969 the Hippies' dream of peace and love darkened into America's nightmare. That afternoon, the Los Angeles police were summoned to a ranch-style mansion in an exclusive suburb of the city where five mutilated bodies had been discovered. The killings had been carried out by disturbed but otherwise apparently ordinary young Americans acting under the demonic influence of their mad messiah, Charles Manson.**

*Manson was not content to be idolized as a man – he demanded to be worshipped as a god.*

In the driveway lay the body of a young man, Steven Parent, who had been shot and stabbed while sitting in his car. On the lawn were the bodies of two more victims, Abigail Folger and Jay Frykowski, both with multiple stab wounds. Frykowski had also been shot twice at close range.

Inside the house the police found two more bodies, those of Jay Sebring, who had also been shot and repeatedly stabbed, and the actress Sharon Tate. Tate, the wife of film director Roman Polanski, the owner of the house, had been eight months' pregnant with their first child. On the walls the murderers had scrawled the words 'Death to pigs' using the victims' blood.

The sickening scene was echoed the following day at a house five miles away in Hollywood where another two bodies, those of supermarket owner Leno LaBianca and his wife Rosemary, were found. It was later learnt that after stabbing the couple, the killers had calmly gone into the kitchen, cut themselves slices of watermelon and drunk their fill of chocolate milk. Before leaving they fed their victims' pets.

> Before leaving the house the killers fed their victims' pets.

The killers' leader, Charles Manson, was the son of a prostitute and had spent the great majority of his life since the age of 11 in boys' homes and various corrective institutions. On his release in spring 1967 aged 32 he had chosen a long distance bus at random. It took him to the Haight Ashbury district of San Francisco, which was then the mecca for America's 'alternative' youth culture, the Hippies.

Manson found it easy to lose himself in the seething community of so-called 'freaks'. He grew his hair long, played the guitar and tried to break into the music business, but nobody wanted to hear his songs. The rejection fed his latent paranoia and the devotion of his female admirers who knelt at his feet and reassured him that his

*Followers of Manson kept a vigil outside the court-house during their 'messiah's' trial.*

himself to be both Satan and Jesus Christ. He had his disciples, whom he called Satan's Slaves, re-enact the crucifixion at regular intervals with him in the leading role, but instead of ascending to heaven he would be untied in time to take part in the obligatory orgy. Later, in the guise of Satan, it was claimed that he would preside over the sacrifice of living animals, but even this did not apperently satisfy his infinite capacity for evil.

Tiring of his followers' slavish adoration, and eager to see just how far he could lead them, Manson devised a series of petty crimes which were to culminate in the horrific Hollywood killings. He later claimed that the victims were a sacrificial offering to Abaddon ('the destroyer'), the demon of the Apocalypse described in the Book of Revelation.

genius would one day be recognized and rewarded. But even this was not enough to satisfy Manson's lust for power and blood.

## DESERT FAMILY

When he set up a commune in the Hollywood Hills they dutifully followed, willingly submitting to his rules, which demanded that they sleep with any man he chose for them. None of his so-called 'Family', who were predominantly female, were permitted to ask why. This word was strictly forbidden. Incredibly, his following continued to grow. A middle-aged admirer was told that she was too old to qualify for the master's attentions, but that she was to leave her 15-year-old daughter, and she obeyed.

Manson was not content to be worshipped as a man; he demanded to be idolized as a god, and proclaimed

*While the Beatles symbolized the search for personal spiritual enlightenment in the 1960s, Charles Manson assumed the role of the Antichrist.*

# MANSON'S APOCALYPSE

As early as 1961 Manson was convinced that America's materialistic society was about to be engulfed in a 'race war Armageddon', or 'helter skelter'. Inflamed by racial hatred and rumours of militant black supremacist groups with hidden armouries, he developed a plan to initiate a series of murders which he hoped to blame on the blacks and then to hide underground while the races fought it out in the streets above.

Encouraged by Manson, the Family identified with the locusts in the Book of Revelation, who would harass 'those men which have not the seal of God on their foreheads'. In anticipation of 'helter skelter' they stole fashionable open-top 'dune buggies', which were to serve as the locusts' 'breast plates of iron and fire', and retreated to a run-down ranch in Death Valley. Eager to discover the 'bottomless pit' described in Revelation, where these creatures would take shelter during the battle, Manson found a likely hole in the desert, but could not afford to have it drained.

# HELTER SKELTER

**Sharon Tate and the other victims of the Family were to be the first sacrifices in a race war which Manson had named 'Helter Skelter', after the Beatles' song of the same name. In his deranged mind Manson alternately assumed the roles of Satan and the Messiah with the Beatles recast as the four horsemen of the apocalypse!**

Manson preached that 'helter skelter' would be a racial war between black and white which the black population would win. In time, according to Manson, the victors would find that they were unable to govern and would appeal to him and his Family to help.

The Family's set text and scripture, such as it was, derived largely from the Beatles' lyrics, which Manson, who often referred to himself the 'fifth Beatle', dissected in the belief that they held secret messages for him and his followers. The lyrics to the song *Piggies* was said to have been taken as justification for the mutilation of the wealthy LaBianca's with a knife and fork, while *Happiness Is A Warm Gun* was taken literally instead of as the sly sexual joke John Lennon had intended. Innocent songs such as *Blackbird* were seen by Manson as endorsing his racial prejudices. He even interpreted the blank cover of the so-called *White Album* as a sign that his racial Armageddon was imminent.

The other text that obsessed him was Chapter 9 of the Book of Revelation, which includes the line 'Neither repented they of their murders, nor of their sorceries, nor of their fornications, nor of their thefts.' This passage, he told his disciples, proved that murder was justified, that death meant freedom for the imprisoned soul. To kill a person at the End of Days, argued Manson, was to free them from earthly torment, and he cited another favourite passage from Revelation in defence of this; 'In those days shall men seek death, and shall not find it; and shall desire to die, and death shall flee them.'

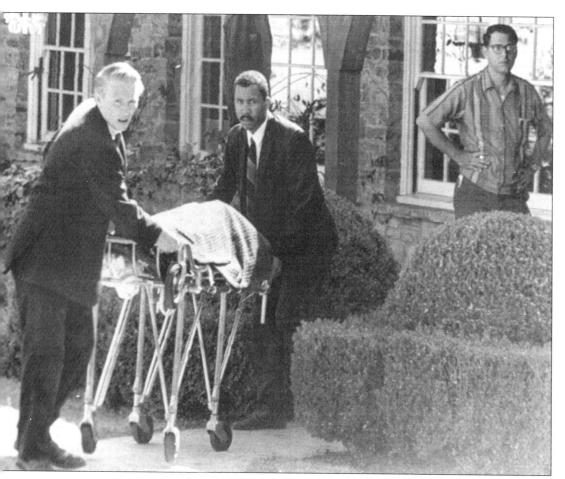

Later, one of the girls convicted of the Tate-LaBianca killings cited this corrupted credo in an attempt to justify the slaying of Sharon Tate. 'I loved her, and in order for me to kill her I was killing part of myself when I killed her ... You have to have a real love in your heart to do this for people.'

Prosecuting attorney Vincent Bugliosi was convinced that the guilty Family members were neurotic psychotics long before they met Manson and that he had simply exploited their neuroses for his own perverted ends. 'Nearly all had within them a deep-seated hostility towards

*The Hollywood killings were regarded by Manson and his disciples as the first 'sacrifices' in a race war.*

*Film actress Sharon Tate was eight months' pregnant when she was murdered by Manson's disciples.*

society and everything it stood for,' wrote Bugliosi 'which pre-existed their meeting with Manson.' He had pandered to their paranoia, 'their latent hatred, their inherent penchant for sadistic violence, focusing it on a common enemy, the establishment. He de-personalized the victims by making them symbols. It is easier to stab a symbol than a person.'

## SLAVISH DISCIPLES

Even as the full horror of the murders unfolded in court, Manson's most ardent disciples remained mesmerized. They shaved their heads and held a silent vigil outside the courtroom.

Inside, their demented Manson played the manipulative messiah to the very last. 'The courtroom is like unto an old useless mannequin smelling with lies, deceit and the strings of graft and corruption,' he declared. 'Mr and Mrs America, you are wrong. I am not the King of the Jews, nor am I a hippie-cult leader. I am what you have made me.'

**'It is easier to stab a symbol than a person.'**

Ater hearing the sentence of death pronounced, he remained defiant, and apparently remains so to this day. 'I am not ashamed or sorry,' he told a British photographer. 'If it takes fear and violence to open the eyes of the dollar-conscious society, the name Charles Manson can be that fear.'

Because of a moratorium on execution in the USA in the early 1970s, Manson is now serving out nine consecutive life sentences at Vacaville penitentiary. It is said that aside from his duties as caretaker of the prison chapel he remains in his cell for fear of being attacked by the other inmates.

# LENNON'S OBSESSION

Manson and his followers believed that their actions had been endorsed by messages hidden in the Beatles' lyrics. This was, of course, nonsense, but John Lennon did have a lifelong obsession with the occult significance of numbers which occasionally appeared in his songs.

Lennon's fatidic number was 9. The Beatles' manager Brian Epstein had discovered the group on 9 November 1961 and secured their first recording contract on 9 May 1962. Lennon met Yoko Ono on 9 November and their son, Sean, shared his father's birthday on 9 October.

The numeric total of the Lennons' apartment (72) in the Dakota Building, New York, and the street on which they lived (West 72nd Street) was also 9. Three of Lennon's songs, *Revolution Number 9*, *One After 909* and *Number 9 Dream* were written at his mother's house at 9 Newcastle Road, Liverpool.

All this might be dismissed as mere superstition on Lennon's part was it not for the fact that he was gunned down outside the Dakota on 8 December, 1980 (9 December in Liverpool) and taken to the Roosevelt Hospital on 9th Avenue. Coincidence or fate?

*John Lennon had a lifelong obsession with the occult significance of numbers. His fatidic number was nine.*

# ARMAGEDDON IN WACO

**The siege of the Branch Davidian cult Headquarters at Waco, Texas, in April 1993 was the final act in their mad messiah's staging of Armageddon. As the FBI closed in at noon on 19 April, the cult's leader, David Koresh, ordered that the building be set on fire then sat and read the Bible as the flames engulfed his followers.**

*With his sect surrounded Koresh initiated his own Armageddon.*

The Branch Davidians were formed in 1931 as a radical splinter group of the Seventh-Day Adventists, a Protestant sect whose central belief is the imminent arrival of the Messiah and the end of the world in 1999. The Davidians established a community in Waco, and from the start actively recruited members from the Adventists, who in general regarded them as an extreme and unwelcome element.

Koresh had taken over the group in the 1980s, after the son of the founder had exhumed the body of his recently deceased mother and declared that he would resurrect her. It was Koresh who reputedly reported the son to the authorities, ensuring the man's incarceration in an institution and giving himself a clear field to take over the sect.

Koresh never tired of telling his followers that his surname in Hebrew meant 'the Sun', the literal equivalent of Cyrus, the founder of Persia and conqueror of Babylon, whose favourite form of entertainment was burning his prison-

*Koresh delighted in the fact that his ancient namesake enjoyed burning his prisoners alive.*

ers alive. The king's one good deed was to free his Hebrew slaves and allow them to return to Jerusalem, hence the complimentary reference to him in the Old Testament which Koresh was fond of quoting.

## SEXUAL INITIATION

Having convinced his devotees of his divinity, Koresh was able to persuade many of his female followers to refrain from sleeping with their husbands and to have sex with him instead. He told them that having sex with him was a symbolic initiation and allegedly even singled out some of the young girls to be his future 'wives'. These children later claimed that they had been given a Star of David to wear to show thay had been chosen by Koresh and that they were forbidden to have sex with any other member of the group.

In all, Koresh fathered eight children (including a son he named Cyrus), two with his legal wife and six with three other women, in an attempt to establish an unbreakable 'family' bond with his followers. All the children in the compound were expected to address Koresh as 'father' and their own parents as 'dogs', but to ensure their strict obedience he is said to have introduced physical punishments as well as exerting psychological pressure and threats of eternal damnation. This was necessary, he told them, because they would soon face the ultimate test. The outside world was evil, a new Babylon, against which they, the righteous, would one day have to fight as the Bible had prophesied.

> The outside world was evil, against which they, the righteous would some day have to fight.

That day came on 27 February 1993, when the ATF (the gun law enforcement agency), suspicious of the group's large armaments purchases, sent agents to search the compound, which had been fortified in anticipation of an attack. A gun battle ensued, in which several agents were killed. The rest retreated to the perimeter and awaited reinforcements. The next day the FBI surrounded the compound and a 51-day siege began. Koresh forbade any of his followers to leave, but on the morning of 19 April, as the FBI closed in for the final assault, some managed to escape in the confusion. Others, it is alleged, were killed by cult members as they tried to escape. In the last moments it is claimed that the remaining children were taken from their parents and drugged as Koresh sat back and read the Bible aloud to the adults. At noon he ordered the buildings to be set ablaze and the final act of immolation reduced all to ashes. The FBI were later criticized for their handling of the siege but it is unlikely that anyone could have prevented this mad messiah from bringing about his own personal Armageddon.

# THE MIDDLE CLASS MESSIAH

The face of David Koresh which smiles enigmatically from family photos is that of an average middle class American teenager, and yet, within a few years he had become the paranoid prophet of an apocalyptic cult. He claimed he was acting out a prophecy which must be fulfilled, but were his actions in any sense predictable?

Although his followers obviously considered him to be charismatic, he was not, it is believed, by nature a strong personality. It appears that he was only able to exert power over those even more insecure and introverted than himself, who mistook his pedantry and stubbornness for conviction.

He professed a detailed knowledge of scripture, but had a very limited understanding of its spiritual significance. For him the biblical prophecies were to be taken literally. Subjugation and sacrifice of the self were deliberately perverted into a doctrine based on martyrdom. With his followers he shared a belief in a greater destiny than that which the world was likely to offer and martyrdom gave meaning to these nihilistic beliefs.

As an offshoot of the Seventh-Day Adventists, the Branch Davidians were already firm believers in the imminent arrival of the Messiah. They were apparently content to entrust their fate to a father figure and Koresh was equally at ease in the role until, nearing the symbolically significant age of 33, he convinced himself that as the illegitimate son of a carpenter he was not only a prophet but the Messiah himself.

# AUM SHINRI KYO

'Greet death without regrets.' (SHOKO ASAHARA)

**On 20 March 1995, at the peak of the morning rush-hour, the Tokyo Underground was crowded to capacity with commuters on their way to work. As a train pulled into Kasumigaseki station, a cloud of noxious, choking fumes enveloped the platform, causing panic and forcing thousands to scramble for safety to the surface. Eleven people were killed and over 5000 injured in the incident.**

As the dead and injured were rushed to nearby hospitals, it quickly became apparent that this was not a tragic accident but a deliberate attack using a deadly poison gas. Several passengers aboard the train claimed to have seen a masked man in sunglasses and elbow-length rubber gloves repeatedly stabbing a package wrapped in newspaper with the point of his umbrella.

Although no one claimed responsibility for the attack, the authorities swiftly concluded that an extreme religious sect, Aum Shinri Kyo ('Supreme Truth'), was behind it. The sect is also believed to have carried out other poison gas attacks, notably on the Yokohama underground a few weeks earlier and at the town of Matsumoto where three judges had been staying while adjudicating in a land dispute involving the group.

## ARCHITECT OF THE GREAT PYRAMID

Aum Shinri Kyo, which reputedly has 10,000 members, had been under surveillance by Japanese security officials for several years following reports of the abduction and intimidation of reluctant disciples and the alleged kidnapping of two eminent lawyers who were attempting to expose their activities. The group's 40-year-old founder, Shoko Asahara,

*Shoko Ashara, the half-blind guru known to his followers as 'the Master'.*

known to his followers as 'the Master', was later arrested and charged with ordering the Tokyo underground attack. Asahara is a half-blind former acupuncturist whom his disciples believe is the reincarnation of Imhotep, the architect of the Great Pyramid. However, in this incarnation he has proven less impressive, abandoning his first sect, the Heavenly Blessing Association, in 1982 after being convicted of selling fake health tonics made from orange peel. His next attempt, the Aum Divine Wizard Association, centred on the promise that it would teach its devotees how to levitate, but it closed down soon afterwards without producing a single graduate. In 1988, Asahara was at it again, founding the

Aum Shinri Kyo sect, for which he allegedly devised masochistic endurance tests, rewarding the chosen by allowing them to drink from a 'Miracle Pond' – the Master's bathwater spiked with hallucinogenics.

## INSTANT ENLIGHTENMENT

It is claimed that in exchange for their money and devotion Asahara promised to lead his followers to enlightenment in preparation for the apocalypse, which he predicted would destroy the world in 1997. He understood that his youthful

*The sect's gas attacks caused panic among early-morning commuters on the Underground system.*

## THE END IS NIGH

The End of the World has been a staple prediction of extreme religious sects since biblical times. Aum Shinri Kyo is just one of 17,000 religious sects currently registered in Japan, many of which predict that the end of the world is nigh and urge the population to reject materialism before it is too late. The one million members of the Reiha-no-Hikari sect, which was established in 1956, regularly pray for up to 14 days at a time to purge themselves of materialist desires in preparation for their premature trip to paradise. The proliferation of these groups in recent years has led to the 1990s being dubbed `the rush hour of the gods'. Asahara predicted that Armageddon would take place in 1997 and that only Aum disciples would be saved, but his followers have also made predictions.

Back in 1991, Masami Tsuchiya, the head of the sect's chemical arms unit, had written in his diary that `Asahara will be imprisoned in the 1990s, but his trial will prove the existence of supernatural power and all 100 million Japanese will become followers of Aum.' He went on to predict that by 1995 the sect would be more powerful than the state and that it would advance into Jerusalem and be tortured by `heretics' in 1998-99. The military might of Aum would then free its followers and after a final world war Tsuchiya would preside over a new Japanese empire that would last 1,000 years.

*Aum Shinri Kyo is just one of the 17,000 sects registered in Japan.*

following had little patience with traditional routes of spiritual discipline and devotion and so he devised bizarre high-tech methods promising instant enlightenment. Members were put on strict near-starvation diets of Aum food, a daily dish of seaweed, radish, carrots and burdock roots. Some were apparently locked in stainless steel cylinders to experience sensory deprivation and others were allegedly drugged. But the most disturbing technique was that known as 'Perfect Salvation Initiation' which required disciples to wear rugby scrum caps wired to batteries around their waists. These 'brain-hats' delivered 4 to 10 volt shocks to 'calm' the brain and activate the chakras, the psychic centres and vital energies within the body connecting the spirit to the higher realms.

> Disciples wore rugby scrum caps wired to batteries.

A police search of the sect's many compounds, following the Tokyo underground attack, yielded 200 tonnes of chemicals used in the production of Sarin, a nerve gas devised by the Nazis, that can kill within minutes. Traces of the chemicals were also found at Kasumigaseki station, leaving little doubt that the group was behind the attack.

However questions remain. If the attack was carried out by members of the sect, what were they hoping to gain? Was it merely an indiscriminate display of power by religious fanatics? Or the first act in their apocalypse? And who is ultimately responsible for such acts — he who orders the murder or the follower who unquestioningly carries it out?

# THROUGH A GLASS DARKLY

T he following pages present indisputable evidence of the existence of precognition - the ability to foresee the future. However, the most intriguing aspect is not the fact that such a phenomenon exists, but rather that the experience varies radically according to the individual.

Nostradamus, the Seer of Salon, was apparently able to foresee events so far into the future that it is arguable that he was able to comprehend what he saw. His descriptions are so vague and of such a cryptic nature as to be a source of intense speculation to this day.

And yet other seers and psychics have foreseen specific events occurring within their lifetime, or limited to their own fate and that of their families with alarming clarity.

Some have attained a certain celebrity by specializing in papal prophecies, presidential assassinations, natural disasters or warfare - all of which they apparently had no prior knowledge of or personal interest in. But the most revealing are the personal premonitions, those isolated incidents which forewarn of danger to a family member, or to the psychic themselves. The frequency of these among 'ordinary' people suggests that precognition is linked to emotion, a 'lost' primal sixth sense for survival.

It seems likely that we are all subject to involuntary precognition, but that these flashes of the future are often confined to our dreams when the rational mind is sleeping and the latent psychic faculties are unhindered by the intellect.

And what of those premonitions which are proclaimed by previously reliable psychics but which do not come true? Are we to dismiss the overwhelming evidence in favour of precognition merely because of a few 'misses', or could there be another explanation for these erratic talents - an explanation which could turn our ideas of time and space on its head?

# THE PAPAL PROPHET

**Despite the proclamation of St Augustine in 400 AD that prophecy was to be considered as heresy, the Catholic Church has seen its share of papal predictions and has been the subject of much prophetic speculation. A twelfth-century archbishop predicted the papal lineage through to the 20th century with uncanny accuracy. Will he be proved equally accurate in his prediction for the end of the world?**

In 1139, while on a visit to Rome, Malachy O'Morgair, the Archbishop of Armagh – later to be canonized as St Malachy – succumbed to a series of involuntary visions during which he 'saw' every single successor to the papal line, from the incumbent Pope Innocent II to the pope of the Apocalypse. St Malachy described most of the one hundred and twelve successors in a manuscript which he entrusted to Pope Innocent II, who ordered that the predictions should be 'lost' among the papal archives. It was not until four hundred years later that they were published, after being accidently discovered by a Benedictine scholar researching the life of their author.

St Malachy described most of the future popes in no more than a sentence, but they are readily identifiable if their background is known. For example, Malachy predicted that a vacant seat in the papacy would be filled by 'a guardian of the hills'. Pope Alexander VII was elected in 1655 and his family crest depicted a star hovering in the heavens above three hills. Malachy noted a later incumbent as a 'rose of Umbria', which might accurately describe Pope Clement XIII who became Pope in 1758 after having resided in Umbria prior to his election. The symbol of Umbria is a rose. Malachy's 'swift bear' could refer to Pope Clement XIV (elected 1769), whose family crest included a running bear, while the 'apostolic wanderer' might be an appropriate description of Pope Pius VI (elected 1775), who was deposed during the French Revolution and hunted for the rest of his life.

One remarkable aspect of St Malachy's predictions is that their accuracy does not appear to diminish the further they are from his own time. One of the first pontiffs of the twentieth century was described by St Malachy as reigning during a period of 'religion depopulated.' What better description could there be of Pope Benedict XV who was elected in 1914 on the eve of the First World War and who would also witness the suppression of 200 million Roman Catholics as a consequence of the Russian revolu-

*St Malachy predicted that Pope John would be the third from last of the pontiffs before the Apocalypse.*

tion in 1917? In more recent years the brief reign of Pope John Paul I was reflected in St Malachy's epithet for the pope 'of the middle moon.' John Paul reigned for just 33 days before his sudden death on 28 September 1978, a date which fell between two full moons.

The prophet's final prediction is that for the pope of the Apocalypse. This prediction differs from all the others in that the pope is named and afforded a lengthy description to signify his importance as the pontiff of the 'last days.'

'In the final persecution of the Holy Roman Church, there shall sit Peter of Rome, who shall feed the sheep among great tribulations. When these have passed, the City of the Seven Hills will be destroyed and the dreadful judge will judge the people.'

According to St Malachy's prediction there are just two popes left to reign after the present pontiff vacates the Vatican. If they each reign for ten years, Peter, the pope of the Apocalypse, will preside over the last days on earth in 2009. The problem with St Malachy's predictions in this respect is that although they appear to match up with a succession of elected pontiffs, it could be argued that their vagueness allows any number of credible interpretations to be put on them.

But before we dismiss his pronouncements completely, it is worth noting that St Malachy correctly predicted the date and hour of his own death.

> **Peter, the pope of the Apocalypse, will preside over the last days on earth in 2009.**

*Pope John Paul, whose sudden death was foreseen by St Malachy in his vision of the 'middle moon'.*

DUFFIELD ROAD
DERBY DE22 1JD

## ANTICIPATING THE APOCALYPSE

The Middle Ages was a period of extremes. More aptly known as the Dark Ages, it witnessed an epidemic of religious fervour, persecution and fear stemming from the widely held belief that the apocalypse was imminent.

The year 1000 AD was the first significant date that medieval Christians anticipated as heralding the Second Coming of Christ, being one thousand years after the birth of Christ. But the Church was not keen to authorize the event, because it would have been tantamount to an admission that the first thousand years of their ministration was deserving of Divine intervention. They need not have worried, however. The first millennium passed without incident.

Undaunted the doom merchants recalculated the apocalypse to begin in 1033 AD, arguing that the crucial date was one thousand years after the crucifixion, and not the birth, of Christ.. When that year also came and went without 'signs and wonders in the heavens', the appearance of the so-called 'Conquest Comet' thirty-three years later, in 1066, gave fresh heart to believers, who cited the Norman conquest of Britain that same year as confirmation that something significant was stirring.

But a battle in Britain was not enough to convince the rest of Christendom that Armageddon was nigh, and so the so called 'Endtime' sects of medieval Europe resorted to scanning the Book of Revelation for clues. Someone hit upon the idea of 1666 as a likely year, it being the millennial year plus 666, the number St John identified as representing the Great Beast of the Apocalypse. But it turned out to be an unremarkable year for all but the English architects and builders who enjoyed brisk business following the Great Fire of London.

A myriad of alternative dates were subsequently proclaimed by the Millennarian sects – and proved to be wrong – but the millennial year 2000 AD is the only date that has sparked serious speculation and excited the curiosity of the general population in over three hundred years.

# NOSTRADAMUS

**The prophecies of the French physician and astrologer Michael Nostradamus (1503-66) have proven extraordinarily accurate over the past 400 years, although the obscure symbolism which characterizes his prophetic verses remain a matter of individual interpretation. His mastery of the secret arts of divination and understanding of the forces which influence the future have earned him the title 'The Prince of Prophets'.**

1999 will be a bad year for those of us who live to see it, at least according to Nostradamus. It is the year of the first global nuclear war.

'In the year 1999 and seven months
From the sky will come a great king of terror:
To bring back to life the great king of the Mongols
Before and afterward Mars reigns happily.'

The last line suggests that the war may grow out of a localized conflict aggravated by a pre-emptive missile strike (the 'great king of terror') and that it will be a protracted war with no definite end or overall victor. The reference to the Mongols infers that it is likely to involve communist China, as the area of central Asia once inhabited by the Mongols is now largely under Chinese rule. Clues to the identity of the other two protagonists are to be found in the following verse.

'When those of the Northern Pole are united together
In the East will be great fear and dread.
One day the two great leaders will be friends
The New Land will be at the height of its powers
To the man of blood the number is repeated.'

The 'New Land' he refers to may well mean America, while the other major power in the northern hemisphere is Russia, although it could also refer to the armies of a united Europe. During the 1980s it was tempting to see the 'man of blood' as Russia's President Gorbachev, due to the bloodstain-like birth mark on his forehead, with George Bush, the American President as the other 'great leader'. But both men have now been sidelined by history. The 'man of blood' is therefore likely to be the third 'Antichrist', the others being Napoleon Bonaparte and Adolf Hitler. The allusion to the Antichrist is emphasized

by the phrase 'the number is repeated', which appears to be a reference to the Book of Revelation in which St John identifies the second Beast as a man whose name has a numerical value of 666. In the context of other verses this 'man of blood' has been identified as a new communist dictator of China who will wage a nuclear war against a Russian-American alliance in the final year of the century.

Today this scenario is not as incredible to imagine as it would have been before the fall of the European communist bloc and the collapse of the Soviet Union. Moreover, Nostradamus' image of the Antichrist as an immoral man and an enemy of humanity, rather than a supernatural

*Napoleon Bonaparte is understood to be the second of three incarnations of the Antichrist foretold by Nostradamus.*

being, is another element which makes his predictions more credible, and therefore more alarming, than the fanciful apocalypses of the Biblically inspired prophets. Nevertheless, the destruction and aftermath of his apocalypse is just as distressing.

'The Great Star will boil for seven days,
Its cloud making the sun appear to have a double image:
The great dog will howl throughout the night...
The parched earth shall wax drier and drier,
And a great flood when it shall appear.'

What makes these and other prophecies of Nostradamus worthy of serious consideration even today is not just his past record for accuracy, but his deeper understanding of the influences which affect the future of the world.

**1999, Nostradamus predicted, will be the year of the first global nuclear war.**

It is a popular misconception that the 'Seer of Salon', as he was known, divined these future events after studying the stars. Astrology is largely based on the alignment of the planets at the moment of a person's birth, and so it is impossible to predict events for a person who has yet to be born. However, nations are also said to be under the influence of stars, which is why it is possible for serious astrologers to predict the mood and potential actions of a particular nation. Germany, for example, was founded as a nation under the sign of Scorpio, and its latent potential for

violence heightened under certain planetary configurations during the 1930s when key figures were in place to exploit the circumstances. However, the key word here is 'potential' – no matter how strong the planetary influences may be, each individual and nation retains the element of free will and thus can alter 'destiny' by changing their behaviour.

Nostradamus understood this, which is why he was able to foretell so many wars and conflicts between peoples of which he could have had no foreknowledge.

*Germany's potential for destruction was exacerbated by the actions of its leaders during the Nazi era.*

## THE SEER OF SALON

The opening quatrains of Nostradamus' first book of prophecies, *The Centuries* (published in 1555) describes one of the methods he used to invoke his visions.

'Sitting alone at night in secret study,
Rested on a brazen tripod,
An exiguous flame comes from the solitude,
Making successful that worthy of belief.
The handheld wand is placed in the midst of the BRANCHES,
He moistens with water his foot and garment's hem,
Fear and a voice makes him quake in his sleeves,
Divine splendour, the divine sits nigh.'

It is the same as that used by the prophets of the Greek Oracle at Didyma, of whom the philosopher Iamblichus wrote, 'The prophetess of Branchus either sits upon a pillar, or holds in her hand a rod bestowed by some deity, or moistens her feet or the hem of her garment with water ... and by these means ...she prophesises.'

Nostradamus appeared eager to give a clue to his methods of divination by highlighting the word 'Branches' to draw the allusion to Branchus, the Greek god of prophecy. And yet he encoded his predictions in cryptic verse rich in obscure symbolism.

It has always been argued that he recorded them in this way to avoid being accused of sorcery, but if this is true why did he openly admit to the practice of prophecy by revealing his methods in the verses quoted above?

It could well be that he deliberately obscured the meaning, so that only those learned in the secret arts could benefit from his foreknowledge. After all, the prophecies were published for the benefit of scholars like himself and not for the entertainment of a largely illiterate public. Moreover, as a wise and educated man he would have been aware of the dangers of proving the existence of predestination to a populace who would then feel they had no influence on the course of history, or even their own lives.

# NOSTRADAMUS — CYCLE OF THE CENTURIES

**In his quatrains, Nostradamus predicted a time of traumatic transition for the end of the twentieth century. Heralded by the reappearance of Halley's Comet the old order will begin to crumble and the human race will be tested by devastating wars and natural disasters. But if we survive into the next century the Millennium will bring a thousand years of peace.**

When Halley's Comet crossed the skies in 1985, many people saw it as the opportunity to witness a once in a lifetime phenomenon, but for those who had studied the prophecies of Nostradamus, the Comet was the portent of profound and dramatic changes.

'After great misery for mankind an even greater one approaches
When the great cycle of the centuries is renewed
It will rain blood, milk, famine, war and diseases
In the sky will be seen a fire, dragging a tail of sparks.'

The renewal of the 'great cycle of the centuries' is a clear reference to the millennium and the mention of past misery to the two world wars which marked the twentieth century as a particularly dark era for the human race,

or perhaps to the great global war of 1999 (see previous pages). The word 'milk' is commonly used in translations of the *Centuries*, but is likely to have been a mistake. The old French word for milk was 'laict' which could have been a misreading of 'laicite', meaning an anti-religious movement. So, Nostradamus appears to be predicting an era of violence, loss of religious faith, famine, war and plagues from 1985 until the end of the century. Recent events suggest he may yet be proven correct.

## THE MILLENNIUM

But what of the year 2000 and beyond? Are we destined to be visited by the spectres of disease and disaster forever, or is there hope for humanity at some time in the future? According to the most widely accepted interpretation of the final quatrains, and the astrological clues Nostradamus himself gives to the timing of these events, we can expect two more wars in the first years of the twenty-first century before an unbroken era of peace which will last a thousand years. Of the first of these wars he has written:

'The Arab Prince, Mars, the Sun, Venus, (in Leo), The rule of the Church will succumb to the sea, Towards Persia very nearly a million (men) The true serpent will invade Egypt and Byzantium.'

*Nostradamus envisaged World War II as an era of 'great misery'.*

*Can the fate of nations be altered by the will of its leaders to make peace instead of war?*

By which we are to understand that a Middle Eastern dictator will encourage an Islamic fundamentalist invasion of Iran (Persia), Egypt and Turkey (Byzantium) after their religion, symbolized by 'the Church', becomes an empty vessel for their religious hatred.

A second, unspecified war breaks out shortly afterwards and ends with the coronation of a new king whose reign will 'bring peace to the earth for a long time'.

After the human race has conquered its fears, controlled its primitive instincts for self-destruction and taken responsibility for its own future, rather than delegated it to a Father-Creator and his earthly representatives – an evolutionary step which Nostradamus symbolizes in the binding of Satan – 'then shall commence between God and man a universal peace. There shall he abide for the space of a thousand years.'

> **We can expect two more wars in the first years of the next century.**

But towards the end of this seventh millennium (Nostradamus had calculated the Creation as beginning in 4137 BC) there will be climactic changes and cosmic cataclysms on such a scale as to render the planet practically uninhabitable. In a letter to King Henry II of France the seer had stated, 'the rains will be so diminished and such an abundance of fire and fiery missiles shall fall from the heavens that nothing shall escape the holocaust. This will occur before the last conflagration'.

It is hard to believe that nations will be capable, let alone willing, to wage war in the wake of a natural global catastrophe, but Nostradamus was convinced of the truth of his vision. In a letter to his ill-fated son, Cesar, he describes the last days of the human race in the year 3797 AD as being initiated by 'the worldwide conflagration which is to bring so many catastrophes and such revolutions that scarcely any lands will not be covered by water, and this will last until all has perished save history and geography themselves'.

So much spurious speculation has been offered as to the 'true' interpretation of these verses that it might be well to note the seers' own warning to those seeking to know the future without having first dedicated themselves to the prophetic and secret arts:

'Let those who read this verse ponder its meaning
Let the common crowd and the unlearned leave it alone
All of them – Idiot Astrologers and Barbarians – keep off
He who does the other thing let him be a priest of the rite.'

*Nostradamus predicted that religious fundamentalism in the Middle East would spark a major war in the new millennium.*

# THE LAST PROPHECY OF NOSTRADAMUS

In common with a number of other seers and psychics, Nostradamus foresaw the date of his own death. But, more remarkably, he correctly predicted the date he would finally be laid to rest – 134 years later!

Shortly before his death in 1566 the seer commissioned an engraver to engrave a metal plate with a date – 1700. Upon the seer's death the plate was placed in his coffin and nothing more was known about it until 134 years later when the coffin was exhumed. The authorities had decided to place the prophet's remains in a more prominent position, but before they reburied it they opened the coffin to make sure the corpse was indeed that of their most celebrated citizen. The skeleton was identified as that of Nostradamus, but as if to satisfy those who doubted his prophetic gifts the metal plate confirmed the date of this bizarre event – 1700.

# MOTHER SHIPTON

**Ursula Sontheil (1488-1561), or Mother Shipton as she became known, was born during a period of English history when her prophetic gifts, hermit-like existence and crone's appearance could have sent her to the stake. Instead, she survived to become a celebrated folk prophet whom popular legend credits with foretelling the invention of the telegraph, railways and the end of the world!**

Local legend has it that Yorkshire's famous prophet was born from the unholy union of a wild orphan girl and a handsome demon. The story goes that the couple courted openly until the locals had the girl brought before the courts on a charge of witchcraft, of which she was later acquitted. On being freed, she discovered that her demon lover had abandoned her and in her anguish she gave birth to a deformed daughter whom she named Ursula. Having entrusted the child to the care of the parish nurse, she took refuge in a convent where she later died of a broken heart.

Ursula's hunchback, rickety legs, bulging eyes and hooked nose proved too much for the nurse, and the little girl was sent away to school. There her grotesque appearance brought taunts from the other children, but Ursula had her revenge by setting invisible demons on her tormentors. Legend this may be, but the facts of Ursula Sontheil's life and the accuracy of her predictions are a matter of record. Ursula became known as Mother Shipton after marrying a local man, Toby Shipton, who was none too happy about his wife being known as the local witch. However, her subsequent fame mollified him

to some degree. At first her predictions were limited to local matters, such as births, deaths, marriages and the prospects for the harvests, but as her reputation grew so did the breadth of her inner visions. As with Nostradamus, who also feared persecution for practising the secret arts, Mother Shipton expressed her predictions in obscure symbolism. A typical verse proclaimed that 'When the English Lion shall set his feet on the Gallic shore Then shall the lilies begin to droop for fear. There shall be much wailing and weeping among the ladies of that country Because the princely Eagle shall join with the Lion to tread all that shall oppose them.'

It is widely understood that this verse refers to the English invasion of France in 1513. The 'English Lion' was a clear reference to King Henry VIII, who attacked France with his ally, Emperor Maximilian of Germany, whose emblem was the eagle. Lilies are the emblem of France and the invasion would certainly have had the fair ladies of France afraid for the fate of their menfolk and their own honour.

Lilies figure in another of Mother Shipton's predictions, that of the trial and execution of Charles I in 1649.

*Mother Shipton's appearance may have been exaggerated to enhance the legend.*

**Such was Mother Shipton's popularity that many predictions were erroneously attributed to her after her death by unscrupulous publishers.**

# THE WAR TO END ALL WARS

Mother Shipton's most dramatic prophecies describe a series of future wars which culminate in the final battle of Armageddon. In three separate predictions she describes the war to end all wars, although she fails to put a date to any of them.

'The Time shall come, when Seas of Blood,/Shall mingle with a greater Flood', runs the first, while the second states, 'Great noise there shall be heard, Great shouts and cries,/And seas shall thunder, lowder than the skyes,/Then shall three lyons fight with three and bring,/Joy to a people, honour to their king.' Could this be an obscure reference to the Allied defeat of the three Axis powers, Germany, Italy and Japan?

The third sounds suspiciously like the London Blitz of World War II with its references to the 'Eagle' (emblem of the Luftwaffe), and an aerial bombardment of London between 'many

*Mother Shipton did not envisage nuclear war but does this invalidate her predictions?*

kingdoms'. However the messianic images, the references to the Land of the Moon and the declaration that the Eagle will be triumphant suggest a possible future war with a new German empire allied to a Middle Eastern regime led by a messianic figure.

'Then shall come the Son of Man, having a fierce beast in his arms, which kingdom lies in the Land of the Moon, which is dreadful throughout the whole world; with a number of people shall he pass many waters and shall come to the land of the Lyon; look for help of the beast of this country and an Eagle shall destroy castles of the Thames, and there shall be a battle among many kingdoms ... and therewith shall be crowned the Son of Man, and the ... eagles shall be preferred and there shall be peace all over the world, and there shall be plenty.'

*Local legend has it that Mother Shipton was the result of union between a wild orphan girl and a handsome demon. The breadth of her visions grew with her reputation.*

'The crown then fits the White King's head who with the lilies soon shall wed; Then shall a peasant's bloody knife. Deprive a Great Man of his life.' Charles had attended his coronation dressed in white and took as his wife the daughter of Henry IV of France. He was beheaded on 30 January 1649 by the common executioner.

Mother Shipton's predictions were not confined to the bloody events of history. She is credited with predicting the invention of the telegraph in the verse, 'Around the world thoughts shall fly In the twinkling of an eye'; and of the railway, 'Carriages without horses shall go. And accidents shall fill the world with woe.' However, such was her popularity, that many predictions were erroneously attributed to her after her death, either by country people looking to preserve their own strange sayings and folk lore, or by unscrupulous publishers eager to sell 'updated' copies of her prophecies. This was the origin of the famous verses relating to the telegraph and the railway; they had, in fact, been the invention of a Mr Charles Hindley, who sought to publish an edition of her 'newly discovered' predictions in 1862. The damage caused by his forgery left an indelible stain on her reputation, but such was her fame among the locals of Yorkshire that they erected a memorial stone near York, which reads:

'Here lyes she who never ly'd,
Whose skill often has been try'd,
Her prophecies shall still survive,
And ever keep her name alive.'

# THE GHOST WRITER

**Whilst the predictions of H.G. Wells and Jules Verne might be categorized as inspired guesses, those of the author Morgan Robertson suggest a paranormal source. Robertson's description of the sinking of a fictional superliner, *The Titan*, in his novel 'Futility' (published in 1898) bears a distinctly disturbing similarity to the tragedy of the *Titanic* which was to occur fourteen years later.**

Robertson was poorly educated and apparently incapable of stringing two sentences together in his normal waking state, and yet, he managed to produce over 200 short stories and several successful novels from the depths of a semi-somnalent trance. He insisted that his prolific output was the result of his mind and body being 'commandeered' by a 'spirit entity with literary ability' - a 'ghost writer' in the truest sense.

An ex-sailor, Robertson had decorated his dingy apartment in New York City to resemble a ship's cabin and here he would lie in a trance as the stories were dictated to him with all the characters finely drawn and the plot tightly structured, ready for him to type up on awakening. Unfortunately, his muse often left him on a whim at a crucial point in the narrative for days or even weeks with no means of inducing the trance so that he could complete the story. It was under such strange circumstances that he was to write what must be the only prophetic novel in literary history.

One evening in 1898 Robertson sank into semi-consciousness and 'dreamt' of a huge modern liner emerging from a dense fogbank somewhere in the Atlantic. It appeared to be about 1000 feet in length and was powered by three propellers which drove it at an incredible 23 knots. As it passed he saw the decks crowded with carefree passengers - at least 2000, more than carried by any known ship afloat, which prompted him to count the lifeboats. There were 24 -

*The Titanic strikes an iceberg just as Robertson had imagined in his novel 14 years previously.*

*Par faim la Pray Fera loup Prisonnier, extreme detresse, la*

*An example of automatic writing dictated by a spirit to a modern medium.*

not enough to save them all. It was then that he heard a voice proclaiming the ship to be 'unsinkable' and noticed the name looming towards him in large letters on the prow – 'The Titan'.

He rose, still drowsy, and began to type a description of what he had seen, adding details of the watertight compartments which would be sealed automatically in the event of flooding to ensure the ship remained afloat.

By the time of its third voyage from New York to England it would be an unrivalled mistress of the sea, rushing heedlessly through the fog before ripping its side open on an iceberg.

**Robertson insisted that his prolific output was the result of his mind and body being 'commandered' by a 'spirit entity'.**

Robertson's ghostly literary partner may have been mistaken in stating that it was the liner's third voyage (although that particular detail may have been down to Robertson himself), but he was unerringly accurate in almost every other respect.

The *Titanic* was indeed almost 1000 feet in length and boasted three propellers and a top speed of 25 knots. It had been heralded as the world's largest liner when it set sail on its fateful maiden voyage from New York to England in April 1912 with just over 2000 passengers on board, all of whom had been reassured that its watertight compartments made it unsinkable. Despite these reassurances the *Titanic* sank with the loss of 1,517 people after striking an iceberg off Cape Race, Newfoundland, on 14 April.

Incredibly, after 14 years of neglect Robertson's novel was inexplicably republished under the new title *The Wreck of the Titan* only months before the real life tragedy.

*Are the apocalyptic visions of science fiction writers channelled involuntarily to prepare us for future disasters?*

**The *Titanic*'s passengers had been assured that the superliner was unsinkable.**

SAINT BENEDICT SCHOOL
DUFFIELD ROAD
DERBY DE22 1JD

# PROPHECY OR PROBABILITY?

The suspicion that Robertson's hand was guided by a spectral scribe with the intention of forewarning the world of the disaster is given some credence by the fact that a number of very similar stories had appeared in magazines and newspapers as early as 1880. In fact, there were so many reported incidents of precognition concerning this particular tragedy that Dr Ian Stevenson Carlson, Professor of Psychiatry at the University of Virginia, made a special study of the phenomenon in the 1960s. Dr Carlson was not convinced that Morgan Robertson's novel was a true case of precognition, but was rather a chance series of coincidences and intelligent guesswork which only proved the laws of probability.

'A writer of the 1890s familiar with man's repeated hubris might reasonably infer that he would overreach himself in the construction of ocean liners ... overconfidence would neglect the importance of lifeboats; recklessness would race the ship through the areas of the Atlantic icebergs; these drift south in the spring, making April a likely month for collision ... Having reached the general conclusion of the probability of such a disaster, inferences ... might fill in details to provide correspondences which would have an appearance of precognition...'

Another explanation is that Robertson's sub-conscious had tapped into Cayce's Universal Mind, at a time when those who were to 'dream up' the *Titanic* were considering the possibility of the project.

# MADAME DE THEBES

One of the most famous French fortune tellers of modern times was Anne Victoire Savary, better known as Madame de Thebes. In 1905 she felt oppressed by a presentiment of doom and published a gloomy forecast for the future of Europe in her annual almanac for that year. 'The future of Belgium is extraordinarily sad,' she wrote. 'This land will set all Europe in flames.'

*Belgian lancers in the capital, Brussels. Madame de Thebes predicted a sad future for their country.*

By 1913 the sense of impending catastrophe was almost palpable, prompting Madame de Thebes to publish a more detailed prediction in a vain attempt to exorcize her unease.

'I see in the hands of distinguished Italians I have studied signs of a war of unprecedented violence ...When it comes, Germany will have desired it; but after that neither Prussia nor the Hohenzollerns will keep their former dominating position. As I have repeatedly emphasized, the days of the Kaiser are numbered, and after him great changes will take place in Germany. I speak of his reign, not of the days of his life.' And of the Prussian Prince she predicted that he would never follow his father to the throne.

A year later, just months before the assassination of the Austrian Archduke in Sarajevo which sparked World War I, she proclaimed, 'The tragedy in the Imperial House of Austria, which was foretold a year ago, will come to pass. No one is able to ward off destiny.'

But it was not only the great figures of history whose futures she could foretell. As a palmist she claimed to be able to predict the personal fortunes of anyone who allowed her to study their hands.

**'This land will set all Europe in flames.'**

Palmistry promises to reveal the true nature of a person's character and their fate by examining the lines, creases, pads, skin colour and texture of the palm - often in association with an astrological analysis.

In the pre-war years Madame de Thebes had been consulted by numerous Englishmen in whose palms she saw portents of violent death and grievous wounds, leading her to conclude that England would be a major player in the coming conflict.

She may have been a remarkable palmist, but she was certainly lacking in diplomatic skills, according to a number of British officers who consulted her in the spring of 1914. She is said to have refused to continue her reading, remarking that in each case the lifeline

# DREAMS OF DANGER

There have been innumerable cases of parents experiencing premonitions of their son's death in battle, sometimes while the son is still a baby. Invariably it is the mother who experiences the dream, or vision, no doubt because the emotional link is stronger due to the psychic bond formed during pregnancy. However, there is evidence that these experiences might not always be presentiments of death, but rather may be warnings of extreme danger offering opportunities of escape.

The German parapsychologist Professor Hans Bender recorded the case of a mother who had been disturbed by recurring dreams of her son, in which he lay in a field with a bullet wound in his neck and a look of extreme terror in his eyes. These nightmares had begun while her son was still a child, but she had dismissed it as the expression of an irrational fear. However, on the night of 8 February 1945, the nightmare was so vivid, and the sense of danger so intense, that she awoke and prayed until the morning, when her fear subsided.

Her son was then serving with the German Army in the Ukraine and it later transpired that on that particular night he had been wounded and taken prisoner by the Russians. The prisoners were being picked out by searchlight and shot one by one when the light fell on the wounded son. Intuitively he cried out for his mother to help him and as he did so the senior Russian officer ordered the killing to stop. The boy returned home two years later.

ended. She did not understand how this could possibly be. The significance of this astonishing coincidence only became clear a short time later. All of the officers who had consulted her were killed in the opening months of the war.

The curious fact concerning prophecy and precognition in wartime is that the anxiety and intensity of living with the prospect of sudden death appears to stimulate the latent psychic faculties of very ordinary people who might normally scoff at the idea of foretelling the future.

A typical case from the files of the Journal for Psychical Research records the experience of a Mrs Munro whose son was serving with the British Army in Palestine. She recounts a dream she had on the night of 26 October 1917 in which she saw her son leap up and clutch his forehead. She looked around for a doctor, but instinctively knew it was hopeless. When she turned to her son again she saw him as he had been at the age of eleven or twelve and at that moment she heard someone cry out, 'It's the ice cream he has eaten which has caused congestion of the forehead.'

Mrs Munro's son was killed on 2 November by a single bullet through his forehead. In an effort to explain her dream she wrote, 'My boy when quite small could never properly enjoy ice-cream because he always said it gave him a pain in the forehead. Dragging this story into my dream seemed to me to be a clever subterfuge on the part of the unconscious, for even in my dream it was quite unconvincing.'

*The assassination of Archduke Franz Ferdinand in Sarajevo sparked World War I.*

# EDGAR CAYCE

**Edgar Cayce (1877-1945), America's celebrated psychic and seer, was known as The Sleeping Prophet, due to his habit of lapsing into a dream-like state from which he derived his psychic insights and invariably accurate predictions. Fortunately, all of his prophecies were carefully recorded and preserved by the association founded in his name, forming a unique testimony to the phenomenon of prophecy.**

The first signs of Edgar Cayce's psychic abilities occurred while he was still a boy in Kentucky. At the age of twelve he casually told his strict Presbyterian parents that he had awoken to see a luminous figure at the bottom of his bed informing him that his prayers had been answered. The following evening, he fell asleep over a grammar book which he had been told to learn before bedtime. In his dream he heard the voice again, but this time it was repeating the words, 'Sleep, and we may help you'. When he awoke, he found that he had unconsciously absorbed every page of the book.

Similar incidents occurred throughout his teens, until his latent talent as a psychic healer manifested itself. At the age of 16, he suffered a serious injury during a game of baseball and was confined to bed. To the surprise of his distraught parents he asked them to make an original form of poultice; this effected a complete cure overnight, although on waking Cayce claimed to have no recollection of having asked them to make it. Other remarkable incidents of intuitive diagnosis and unconventional cures for friends and family followed this, leading eventually to his being recognized as one of the most successful psychic healers in the world.

Sometimes a patient would not even have to be present for Cayce to make a diagnosis. Often the cures he prescribed were obscure specialized compounds of which even experienced physicians were unaware. On one notable occasion, he prescribed a drug called Codiron and named the company who had developed it, but when the patient contacted the company he discovered they had only chosen a name for the drug an hour before!

## UNIVERSAL CONSCIOUSNESS

It seems that Cayce had somehow tapped into a pool of collective knowledge which he called the Universal Consciousness. This might even explain how a staunchly orthodox Christian like Cayce, who did not believe in reincarnation, was able to diagnose problems resulting from his patients' past lives, although it can not explain how he was later able to predict their future. This latter talent developed from his habit of giving financial forecasts to businessmen, many of whom profited from his predictions. Cayce himself had no interest in gaining financially from his gift, maintaining that he would always return his consultation fees if a patient did not benefit from his diagnosis.

On 5 March 1929, and again on 6 April, he warned a client of a downward movement of long duration in the value of stocks and shares. This seemed unnecessarily alarmist as the financial markets in the United States had been enjoying a speculative boom for almost two years,

*Cayce believed he could tap into a pool of collective knowledge.*

*Right: Cayce apparently foresaw the danger to world peace in the alliance between Nazi Germany and Italy in 1936.*

*Below: The Spanish Civil War, begun in 1936, gave the German Luftwaffe the opportunity to rehearse for World War II.*

but Cayce's prediction was proved correct by the Wall Street Crash of late October when 29 million shares were sold over five days in a financial panic which was to lead to wholesale bankruptcy, mass unemployment and the Great Depression.

After his prediction became public he was asked to forecast the principal world events for the next 50 years. This request prompted the following reply, 'This had best be cast after the great catastrophe that's coming to the world in '36 in the form of breaking up of many powers that now exist as factors in world affairs'. Again he was proved correct, as 1936 saw the outbreak of the Spanish Civil War which Nazi Germany used as a rehearsal for World War II. It was also the year in which Italy invaded Abyssinia and Hitler ordered the occupation of the Rhineland. All were critical opportunities for the world's democratic countries to stem the tide of fascism, but they lacked the will to do so.

> He once prescribed a drug which had only been invented an hour before.

# THE FATAL YEAR

According to Edgar Cayce, 1936 would not only be a year of political crisis, but also a physical turning point for the world. He foresaw a shift in the equilibrium of the earth during that year, with 'consequential effects' to be felt around the globe over the following decades.

The fact that scientists have not yet confirmed an alteration in the equilibrium of the earth, or that we have not yet witnessed the dramatic climactic changes that might be expected to result from such an occurrence, does not necessarily mean that it is not happening. There would be a delay between a shift in the equilibrium and the physical effects, some of which would be similar to those we are experiencing in the 1990s, although these are widely accepted as the results of global warming. The shock waves would gather momentum until they affected the position of the Poles, resulting in widespread flooding of the eastern coast of America, northern Europe and much of Japan. In 1934, Cayce forecast a global flood fitting this description and foresaw a reversal of climactic conditions such as we are now witnessing, as a prelude to a shift of the Poles, together with a dramatic increase in volcanic activity. He could not be drawn into giving a date for the climactic flood, but repeatedly proclaimed the years 1958-98 as the crucial years of climactic change.

# EDGAR CAYCE — PROPHECY OR PROBABILITY?

**Edgar Cayce was as entranced by the wonder of his prophetic gifts as were those who witnessed his pronouncements. Throughout his life he maintained that his abilities were 'a gift from God' and yet he was curious enough to speculate as to how it was possible for a mere mortal to foresee the future – and for what purpose.**

Cayce could never understand why he, a simple Sunday School teacher, should have been singled out to be one of the first prophets of the New Age. The answer is that he was probably not singled out as such, but that as with all the genuine prophets, psychics and seers throughout history, he had awoken latent psychic abilities which we all share. As a child, his preoccupation with the Bible and, in particular, the books of the prophets, must have acted as a catalyst on his overactive imagination and stimulated his latent psychic abilities. On waking, his conscious mind then interpreted these visions in the only way he could understand them, in the light of his religious background and beliefs. Cayce was not as pedantic and inflexible as were many of his predecessors. He was fascinated by the realization that the Christian belief in Paradise, which he adhered to, appeared to be contradicted by his visions of past lives and dreams of future incarnations.

Often his trances would reveal that a patient's problems had originated in a previous life and that they would continue to be plagued by the same ailment or personality trait from one incarnation to the next until they had resolved the problem. Recent research by hypnotherapists and psychic researchers using past life regression techniques also suggests that we may carry over our conflicts with other people from life to life until we resolve them, thereby freeing each other of the 'karmic burden'. Cayce did not go this far, as his Christian upbringing prevented him from fully embracing Eastern beliefs. However, it is interesting to note that he was forced to accept

*Cayce explained floods, such as this one in India in 1996, as resulting from shifts in the earth's axis.*

*Did Cayce correctly predict the Kobe earthquake of January 1995 or did he gamble on the law of probability to provide such a disaster?*

this premise in principle following his own experiences under self-imposed hypnotic trance.

## THE AKASHIC RECORD

While reincarnation and memories of previous lives may help explain how Cayce and others were able to make correct psychic diagnosis, it does not explain the phenomenon of the Universal Consciousness, which is closely connected with prophecy and prediction. For this, Cayce considered the existence of what is known in the esoteric tradition as the Akashic record, sometimes called the 'world memory'. This is believed to be a field of energy on the astral plane which retains the image of every event in history together with the thoughts of all living things.

The astral plane is said to be the next level of existence beyond our material world and is the plane of emotion. The emotional effect of violent events would leave impressions at this level just as a flash of intense light leaves an impression on photographic film which psychics and sensitive subjects can see as 'ghosts'. Our deepest thoughts also leave impressions and this might explain how Cayce was able to locate cures of which he would not have been aware of in his waking state. They would be 'on file' in the Akashic record for him to find when his consciousness was raised to that more refined level.

**Cayce believed in the existence of a world memory.**

However, his apparent ability to foresee the future, or more accurately, a potential future, might be explained by the existence of a second Akashic record elsewhere in the ether (see box).

*Are events such as the Kobe earthquake predetermined by a pattern in the ether?*

## DATING THE FUTURE

Cayce has been called one of the first prophets of the New Age - although he preferred to call it 'The Day of the Lord' when 'those who are His' have created the right conditions for the spiritual millennium, the 'Age of Understanding'. The interesting aspect of Cayce's Christian Millennium is that he predicted that it had no definite time scale, but would commence when mankind had created the right conditions. He believed that, as with other future events, the pattern, or plan for change is in place somewhere in the ether, but only mankind's actions will determine the timing.

This could explain why genuine psychics and seers can give very specific, verifiable details for future events, which take place as forecast, but not at the appointed hour. It might also explain why events forecast by previously reliable prophets fail to occur at all.

A fundamental mistake made by those eager to prove that it is possible to predict the future is to assume that the future is preordained. If that were so, we would all be running through a script to a predestined end with no point or purpose to life. Is it not more likely that prior to birth we are all shown the pattern of our life to come, but are then given the free will to act in accordance with our intuition, our 'better nature', or to lose our 'true selves'? We would have opportunities to change the future and amend the pattern which the seers have seen, just as we might choose, on a whim or out of a spirit of adventure, to take an unfamiliar route when we come to a cross-roads. It is only because most of us take the safe, familiar route, thinking and acting on a very material, 'worldly' level, in a predictable way, that so many predictions are accurate.

# THE ASTROLOGER AND THE ANTI-CHRIST

**Adolf Hitler and his inner circle were reputed to be obsessed with predictions, prophecies and the occult. In fact, the Nazis banned the publication of all astrological predictions pertaining to Hitler and the party hierarchy, after some had proven uncomfortably accurate.**

In 1923 Frau Ebertin, a well-known German astrologer, received a letter from a stranger in Munich. The writer was a member of a new radical political party based in Bavaria, and she wanted Frau Ebertin to cast the horoscope for the party's leader, whose identity she refused to reveal. Given his birth date, but no other details, Frau Ebertin consulted her charts and published the result in the 1924 edition of her annual almanac. 'A man of action born on 20 April 1889, with Sun in 29 degrees Aries at the time of his birth, can expose himself to personal danger by excessively uncautious action and could very likely trigger off an uncomfortable crisis.

His constellations show that this man is to be taken very seriously indeed; he is destined to play a "Führer-role" in future battles. It seems that the man I have in mind, with his strong Aries influence, is destined to sacrifice himself for the German nation, also to face up to all circumstances with audacity and courage, even when it is a matter of life and death, and to give an impulse, which will burst forth quite suddenly, to a German Freedom Movement. But I will not anticipate destiny – time will show but the present state of affairs at the time I write this cannot last.' The subject of the horoscope was Adolf Hitler, who fulfilled the first part of the prophecy when he led a failed *putsch* against the Bavarian State Government a few months after the prediction was made.

Although Hitler was sentenced to five years' imprisonment, his long-term ambitions were greatly aided by the reckless and ill-conceived coup attempt. He was able to hijack his trial for propaganda purposes and the resulting publicity did his cause no harm at all.

It also brought Frau Ebertin into personal contact with the Nazi leader,

*Frau Ebertin predicted that the destiny of Germany and Hitler were inter-dependent.*

whom she later described as shy and self-conscious when away from the public, but 'like a man possessed' when he was delivering a speech. After she had finally been trusted with the full details of Hitler's birth, she cast another, more detailed horoscope, which led her to conclude: 'It will turn out that recent events will not only give this movement [the Nazi party] inner strength, but external strength as well, so that it will give a mighty impetus to the pendulum of world history.'

## TIMELY WARNING

Other German astrologers cast far less favourable forecasts, prompting the Nazis to suppress all personal predictions pertaining to the leadership after they seized power in 1933. This edict did not, however, prevent the renowned Swiss astrologer, Karl Ernst Krafft, from casting Hitler's horoscope in the autumn of 1939. What he saw there compelled him to contact Dr Heinrich Fesel, a senior official in Himmler's secret intelligence service.

**Frau Ebertin predicted Hitler would play a Führer-role.**

In a letter which Fesel received on 2 November, Krafft stated that the stars showed that the Führer's life would be threatened the following week by an assassination attempt involving explosives. Fesel, fearful of annoying Hitler, refused to relay the warning, but was called to account six days later after a bomb exploded in a Munich beer hall where the Führer and other high ranking Nazi officials had gathered to commemorate the 1923 Putsch. Hitler would almost certainly have been killed had he not left earlier than expected; the device had been planted in a pillar behind the speaker's podium. This incident is surely a good example of predestination being 'amended' by individual free will, only on this occasion with catastrophic consequences for the rest of humanity.

Krafft was anxious to be given credit for his prediction and unwisely sent a telegram direct to Hitler's deputy, Rudolf Hess. Hess showed Hitler the telegram, following which Krafft was arrested and grilled by the Gestapo who took a long time to be convinced that the astrologer was not personally involved in the assassination attempt.

Frau Ebertin's fate offers a curious postscript to these predictions. She was killed in an air raid in 1944,

having refused to leave her home despite the danger. According to her son, she knew that an air raid was imminent and she also knew which of her neighbours would be killed as a consequence of it, because she had at one time or another cast all their horoscopes. But she refused to leave her hometown because the townspeople had a saying, 'As long as Frau Ebertin is here nothing serious can happen to us'. The astrologer had been trapped by the unerring accuracy of her own predictions.

## NOSTRADAMUS AND THE NAZIS

It is very tempting to interpret various quatrains from the prophetic *Centuries* of Nostradamus to foretell the rise and fall of Hitler's Third Reich. For example, there is the oft-quoted verse, 'Hunger maddened beasts will make the streams tremble; Most of the land will be under Hister; In a cage of iron the great one will be dragged, When the child of Germany observes nothing.'

However there are other, equally plausible interpretations. The verse could be a description of the decline of Venice, with Hister referring to the Danube (Ister was the river's classical name). This is plausible given the repetition of 'Hister' in another, less ambiguous verse; 'In a place not far from Venus [Venice], The two greatest ones of Asia and Africa, Of the Rhine and Hister will be said to come.'

Other verses are less ambiguous:
'In the farthest depths of Western Europe; A child will be born of a poor people, Who by his speeches will seduce great numbers; His reputation will grow even greater in the eastern domain.'

And what of the verse which appears to foretell the German occupation of much of Europe as a consequence of the Nazi Blitzkrieg?
'He will transform into Greater Germany; Brabant, Flanders, Ghent, Bruges and Boulogne.'

Even the Nazi adoption, and inversion, of the hooked cross, or Swastika, an ancient spiritual symbol, appears to have been foreseen by the Seer of Salon.

'The great Priest of the party of Mars; Who will subjugate the Danube [ie, Hitler's annexation of neighbouring Austria]; The cross harried by the crook.'

*The prophecies hidden in Nostradamus's quatrains appear to forewarn of Hitler's aggressive ambitions.*

# PROPHECIES AND PROPAGANDA

**On 10 May 1941, the eve of Germany's invasion of Russia, Hitler's deputy, Rudolf Hess, made a surprise flight to Scotland on an abortive 'peace mission' and was subsequently imprisoned by the British. The Nazis dismissed his action as a symptom of insanity, inflamed by his obsession with astrology, but in truth all sides were fabricating prophecies for propaganda purposes.**

*Hitler's deputy Rudolf Hess made his ill-fated flight on the advice of his astrologer.*

It had long been rumoured that Hess had been Hitler's astrologer and that his predictions up to March 1941 had proven consistently correct. In the late spring of that year, after the German military machine had conquered most of Europe and was looking ambitiously eastward, Hess had reputedly detected signs in the stars that Hitler's fortunes would fade.

His flight had taken everybody by surprise; everybody, that is, with the apparent exception of a British newspaper columnist, an astrologer with the pen name of Gypsy Petulengro, who only the day before had predicted, 'Hitler's right hand man will be lost this week.'

Back in Germany the Gestapo rounded up all known astrologers, including Ernst Schulte-Stathaus, an amateur stargazer and subordinate to Hess, who was suspected of having encouraged his chief's ill-fated adventure. Schulte-Stathaus initially denied fuelling Hess's delusions, but it later transpired that he had informed Hess that 10 May would be a significant date due to the alignment of a major conjunction. It was certainly a memorable date for both men. Hess was imprisoned from that day until his death in 1987, while Schulte-Stathaus was incarcerated by the Nazis for his part in the affair until 1943.

Ironically, it has since emerged that Schulte-Stathaus was not Hess's official astrologer. That dubious privilege was held by a Munich physician, Dr Ludwig Schmidt, whose assertion that a critical conjunction of the planets at the end of May and the beginning of June 1941 would signify a threat to the Führer, was the deciding factor in Hess's otherwise inexplicable flight.

## DESTINED TO FAIL

A more significant figure was Himmler's personal astrologer, Wilhelm Wulf, who had foretold the failure of the Munich *putsch* in 1923. It was his accurate divination of the location of the abducted dictator Benito Mussolini in July 1943 that finally brought him to the attention of the SS supremo.

According to Wulf's reading of Hitler's horoscope, which he had revised and consulted repeatedly over a

## PROPAGANDA AND PLANETS

Both sides in World War II made cynical use of the public's preoccupation with planetary predictions and Hitler himself was reputedly obsessed with astrology.

The Allies enlisted the help of astrologer Louis de Wohl, who toured America in 1941 foretelling Hitler's imminent death, in the hope that news of his prediction would filter back to Berlin. In retrospect, his reading of Hitler's horoscope was otherwise surprisingly perceptive. Comparing Hitler's horoscope to that of Napoleon, he concluded that they shared the same alignment of Saturn, suggesting that Hitler would die or be overthrown within a few years. He also predicted the violent death of Hitler's mistress, although at the time no one even knew of her existence outside Hitler's inner circle. And he foresaw defeat for the German Army on the Russian front, despite the fact that the campaign had just begun and showed all the indications of being another lightning victory for the forces of the Wehrmacht.

De Wohl later wrote fake predictions for counterfeit copies of a popular German astrological magazine, *Der Zenit*, which were printed in England and smuggled into Germany. The trick was to convince the Germans that the magazine's prophet was uncommonly accurate in his predictions, which they did by printing the predictions several months after the events had taken place. The hope was that those who were fooled into believing that the magazine was genuine would then be demoralized by other, fictitious, predictions of crushing defeats for Germany.

The Nazis, too, are known to have planted agents in neutral countries whose sole purpose was to write fictitious horoscopes and articles predicting future victories for the armed forces of the Third Reich. In 1940 the Luftwaffe dropped fake verses from the prophecies of Nostradamus on enemy cities, a trick which was so successful that the allies used it to their advantage soon afterwards.

*Allied astrologer Louis de Wohl compiled what were supposed to be fake forecasts in which he accurately predicted Hitler's death.*

*The surprise victories of the German blitzkrieg were apparently foretold by an anonymous astrologer.*

twenty-year period, the Führer would die a violent but mysterious death in the spring of 1945 in the company of a woman. This appeared to be confirmed by two horoscopes which were in Himmler's possession, but whose author remains unknown. The first was a personal horoscope for Hitler drawn up on 30 January 1933 and the second for Germany prepared on 9 November 1918. Incredibly, both foretold a second war beginning in 1939, with victories for Germany until 1941 followed by a series of reversals culminating in a crisis in the first half of April 1945. August would bring peace and then a period of reconstruction until a new era would begin for the nation in 1948.

**According to Wulf the Führer would meet a violent end.**

These and Wulf's own predictions of Hitler's death and the eventual defeat of Germany in the spring of 1945 prompted Himmler to ask him what might be done to alter the inevitable, but Wulf could only comment that the momentum of events prevented anyone from altering the course of the war, or the Führer's fate. The only possibility, Wulf hinted, was for Himmler to instigate a coup while his stars were in the ascendant and Hitler's were unfavourable, thereby altering the details, but not the overall outcome. The suggestion is that the fate of nations and of individuals are influenced, rather than determined, by the constellations. In this instance, Himmler failed to exploit the opportunity and he followed his Führer down the road to self-destruction.

# THE 'JINX'

**During World War II a London factory worker gained a reputation as a forecaster of disaster. He was plagued by involuntary visions of death and destruction which saved his life on numerous occasions, but which were ignored by his fellow workers. Can we, too, afford to ignore his dire warnings of more wars in the future?**

When in November 1918 London schoolboy Cyril Macklin was told by his history teacher that the Kaiser had just abdicated he piped up that another man was destined to lead Germany and that he would 'raise hell'. In 1927 Macklin saw a picture of this future leader in a newspaper and told his friends, 'That's the man who will cause a world war in 1939.' The photograph showed the then relatively unknown leader of the National Socialist German Workers' Party, Adolf Hitler, barely distinguishable in a large group.

A year later, with no prospect of war in sight, Macklin was struck by a vision of the German Luftwaffe dropping bombs on London and recorded the names of the streets which would be demolished by the Blitz.

By 1940 the Blitz was a reality and Macklin was employed in an aircraft factory, but he did not stay long. During a lunch break he was overcome by nausea and deafened by a loud noise like the throbbing of an aircraft engine, although none was being tested at the time. As the noise grew almost unbearable Macklin felt that he was going to lose consciousness and it was at that moment that he had a vision of the factory in ruins and his friends dead and dying all around him. Unfortunately, nobody that he told took his warning seriously, but for Macklin it was too real an experience to dismiss as imagination. He handed in his notice and left, only days before a German air-raid destroyed most of the factory and killed his friends.

His next job was in a tank factory where he volunteered to take on extra duties as an air-raid warden. During a practice drill he was sitting in an underground shelter when he had an horrific vision of the mutilations caused by a

*Macklin identified Hitler as the future warlord when the Nazi dictator was still an obscure political activist.*

*Before the war Macklin had a vision of the London Blitz and identified the streets that would be bombed.*

deflected aerial torpedo which he 'saw' crash through the roof of the machine shop and slide down the steps into the shelter. Again he gave in his notice and left, only to hear that soon afterwards the factory had suffered a direct hit and that the survivors had described the scene just as he had imagined.

His next job was cut short after an inner voice warned him not to go to work – by now he did not need convincing. The next time he saw the factory it was a smouldering ruin.

> His next job was cut short after an inner voice warned him not to go to work – by now he did not need convincing.

When he arrived at his final wartime workplace he found that his reputation had preceded him. Everyone was on edge and they did not have long to wait until this most ordinary of oracles predicted the wholesale destruction of their factory. By lunch time on his first day Macklin had predicted that the Luftwaffe would strike that very night, dropping a couple of bombs just outside the gates, two more in a fuel bunker and the last near the canteen although the last would fail to explode. He was proved right yet again.

For those who thought that the dropping of the atom bomb meant the end of global warfare, Macklin had more bad news. He forecast two more conflicts in the coming century, though he refused to give further details. But he had a vision of hope, too, in that he saw the divided nations of the world resolve their differences and unite under a single global government sometime in the next millennium.

# THE SPY WHO NEVER WAS

Macklin's visions were involuntary, but there have been incidents of people having what might be called 'unconscious premonitions' - glimpses of the future which they ignore because they do not recognize them as such.

In 1944, just weeks before the Allied invasion of Normandy, the Allied security service were alarmed to discover that the secret code words for the landing points, secret weapons and even the operation itself had appeared as answers in the crossword of a national newspaper. Fearing a security leak, they quizzed the composer of the crossword, Leonard Dawe, who was a schoolmaster with no connections to the military or security services. Satisfied and relieved, the investigators dismissed the incident as an uncanny coincidence, but with so many critical codewords appearing in the mind of one man it might suggest an unconscious premonition by Dawe. Or perhaps Dawe had unwittingly drawn on that collective pool of knowledge, the Universal Consciousness, identified by Edgar Cayce.

Most of us experience *deja vu* from time to time - when we are in a new situation but we have the feeling that we have been in it before, or of visiting a location that is familiar but which we know that we have not been to before, at least in this lifetime.

A clue to this phenomenon might be gleaned from a recent series of controlled experiments in which groups of people with no previous psychic experience were woken from sleep at a critical moment of the cycle and asked what they had been dreaming. Some recalled a precognitive dream which would normally have been forgotten on waking or dismissed as a trick of the imagination if a feeling of *deja vu* occurred some time later.

*Would the Allied invasion of Europe have been necessary if the forewarnings of Macklin and others had been taken seriously?*

# MARIO DE SABATO

**The French psychic and seer Mario de Sabato (b. 1933) has an independently assessed prediction accuracy rating of 85-90 per cent, and yet his most dramatic prophecy, that of a world war with China as the prime aggressor, fortunately failed to materialize at the appointed hour. What does this inconsistency reveal about the unpredictable nature of prophecy?**

The most ardent admirers of de Sabato would have us believe he walks in the steps, but not the shadow, of Nostradamus. For like his fifteenth-century counterpart he too has dedicated his life to the prophetic art independently of religious or national interest and with scant consideration for recognition or reward. Although a devout Catholic he has resisted the temptation to interpret his darker visions as confirmation of the scriptures, reporting instead the simple facts of what he has seen. So convinced is he of the truth of his visions -particularly that of a new Golden Age beginning in the twenty-second century which will be free from the influence of orthodox religion -, that he has risked the displeasure of the Church in order to keep faith with what he considers to be a God-given gift.

His reputation is built on the accuracy and detail of prophecies he made in 1971, when he foretold the political crisis that plagued Italy through the 1980s, culminating in the fall from power of Premier Silvio Berlusconi. He also foretold the series of floods which wreaked havoc across the country in the early 1990s; the fall of the Shah and the Iranian revolution; American military defeat in Vietnam; the civil wars in Angola and Mozambique; the first forays into heart transplant surgery, and even Britain's efforts to join the European Community and its later dispute with the EU over the ban on British beef in 1996-97.

It is not a difficult task for the intelligent, modern prophet who is well-read in world affairs to make an educated guess at the course of events, particularly in historical hot spots such as the Middle East. But de Sabato provides a few extra details that defy the cynics to question his integrity. For example, in the early 1970s he predicted that the West would be virtually crippled in an economic war with the Arab states from which it would take the best part of a decade to recover. Few economists could have foreseen the oil crisis of 1974 to which he must have been referring because it

*De Sabato's psychic impressions of the future suggest that Saddam Hussein may be assassinated in the first years of the new century.*

**The most ardent admirers of de Sabato would have us believe he walks in the steps, but not the shadow, of Nostradamus.**

*De Sabato's reputation as a seer rests on an incredible series of predictions, including the fall of the Shah of Iran.*

was an unprecedented act by a previously disunited group who were reacting to a chain of otherwise disconnected events.

Incredibly, de Sabato also foresaw the long-term outcome of this uneasy alliance. He foretold the war between Iraq and the yet-to-be-declared state of Iran, and also of Iraq's invasion of Kuwait in 1991 with a description of the burning oil fields which would become such a memorable image of the Gulf War.

Remarkably, he also predicted war in Yugoslavia twenty years before the first signs of serious unrest were felt in that country, although he saw Russia as the invader who would be forced to grant autonomy to the self-determining states that would form after the cessation of hostilities. This 'mistake' is interesting because it suggests that accuracy is dependent on the clarity of the vision and not the power of the prophet. De Sabato appears to have confused two violent events (the civil war in Yugoslavia and the guerrilla war against the Russians by the Chechniyan separatists) which roughly took place during the same period. Or perhaps he misinterpreted as openly hostile images the military support which the Russians would give to the Serb forces during the war. It seems incredible that with his record for accuracy he would have risked his reputation on a wild guess at a

**De Sabato's accuracy has made him one of the most remarkable seers of modern times.**

future conflict between these unlikely combatants just for dramatic effect.

De Sabato's accuracy and the descriptive detail he gave so many years in advance have made him one of the most remarkable seers of modern times. And yet, his most dramatic prediction of a third world war breaking out sometime between 1972 and 1982, has proven to be false. So too has his assertion that Germany would never be reunited, while his adamant belief in the arrival of messianic visitors from a distant planet between 2003 and 2031 AD has undermined his credibility with the critics and the cynics. Surprisingly, though, it has not soured his reputation. Once a seer has proven the possibility of precognition and future sight, it seems that considerable allowances will be made for his or her 'mistakes'. The simple fact is that many people want to believe in the predictability of the future because it helps them to make sense of the present.

# DE SABATO'S PREDICTIONS

According to de Sabato, the Middle East will continue to be a source of unrest and tension into the new millennium. A series of military coups will alter the balance of power in the region, beginning with Saudi Arabia, Syria and Lebanon. An unnamed Arab conqueror, who could yet prove to be Saddam Hussein, will be the first Arab ruler of the new century to be assassinated, followed by Libya's Colonel Gaddafi. As the Arab states become stronger Israel will become embroiled in a series of wars leading to its eventual defeat and the occupation of much of its territory. As a result many of Israel's inhabitants will lose heart and emigrate, but will return

once the peace has been made permanent with the Palestinians established in an independent homeland. But de Sabato does not say which country will have to give up its land to accommodate the Palestinians - the very point which is currently preventing this event from taking place.

Europe, too, though economically united under the banner of the EU, will not be free of dissent and unrest. A popular political revolt in Spain will unseat King Juan Carlos, while Britain will dissolve the monarchy after the death of Charles, currently the Prince of Wales, and declare itself a republic.

# JEANE DIXON — THE HIGH SOCIETY SEER

**American psychic Jeane Dixon became a chat show celebrity and the prophet to a President after dramatically predicting the assassination of John F. Kennedy in 1963. Millions of Americans regularly read her predictions in a syndicated newspaper column and thousands more wrote to her from around the world asking her advice on their future, addressing their letters simply to 'Jeane Dixon, USA'.**

When devout Catholic Jeane Dixon knelt in church to pray one day in 1952 she found herself staring not at the altar, but at an outline of the White House. It was as if she was dreaming and yet she was fully conscious and aware of her surroundings. In her vision a slim, blue-eyed young man with short brown hair stood in front of the building with the date 1960 superimposed over them both, as might be seen on a cinema screen. As she looked on, an inner voice announced that a Democrat would be elected President in 1960 and that he would be assassinated while in office.

When the Democrat candidate John F. Kennedy was duly elected in 1960, Jeane consulted a crystal ball which she had been given as a childhood gift by a gypsy woman. The woman had been convinced that Jeane was blessed with the power of prophecy, though as Jeane stared into the ball she prayed the gypsy had been mistaken. But there in the glass, as clear as in a mirror, she saw the White House enveloped in a large black cloud.

Even after the death of the Kennedy's infant son, Patrick, in the summer of 1963, Jeane remained convinced that the black cloud over the White House was a sign of the President's imminent assassination. Her warnings went unheeded by close friends of the Kennedy family who refused to pass them on, knowing that the President would not alter his plans on the advice of a clairvoyant.

When the first news reports came through on the afternoon of 22 November 1963 that Kennedy had been shot in Dallas it was believed that he had only been wounded, but Jeane Dixon knew that he was dead. 'I have never had anything overpower me like this vision,' she said later. Despite her premonition having proven to be genuine, no one close to the Kennedy family would convey her warnings a few months later to the youngest brother Edward when she told them he would shortly have an accident in a private aeroplane. This time the prediction came true the very next day, with the young Senator being seriously injured in a plane crash.

## THE SECOND BROTHER

Incredibly, that was not her last psychic contact with the ill-fated Kennedy clan. The fate of Robert Kennedy, who, ironically, was reluctant to follow his late brother to the

*Jeane Dixon claims to have foreseen events in a crystal ball given to her by a gypsy woman.*

*Dixon's much publicized prediction of Kennedy's assassination brought her instant notoriety.*

White House, was foretold by Jeane Dixon in the most curious circumstances. She was answering questions on precognition and prophecy at a convention in the Ambassador Hotel in Los Angeles in May 1968 when someone asked about Robert's presidential prospects. Before she could answer a black cloud descended in front of her. 'He will never be President,' she announced on recovering her composure, 'because of a tragedy that will take place right here in this hotel.' A week later, on 5 June, Robert Kennedy was shot in the Kitchens of the Ambassador Hotel and died the following day.

**Jeane claims to have foreseen the death of Marilyn Monroe in a spontaneous psychic flash.**

As a celebrity and high society hostess, first in Los Angeles and later in Washington, Jeane found herself in a unique position to foretell the fate of the rich and famous – which she did with unfailing accuracy, her crystal ball hidden under her luxurious mink coat.

On meeting film star Carole Lombard, she was overwhelmed by a sense of foreboding and warned the actress not to travel by plane for the next six weeks. Lombard ignored her advice and was tragically killed in a plane crash within days. During World War II she reputedly became a psychic consultant to President Roosevelt and was quite candid with him when he asked her how long he had left to live. 'Take good care of the ball,' he would say when she bade him goodbye. But not all of her visions appeared in the crystal ball. Jeane claims to have foreseen the death of Marilyn Monroe - whom she had never met - in what she later described as a spontaneous 'psychic flash', suggesting that such visions can be due to a certain empathy with the subject, even if they are complete strangers.

On the subject of world affairs she predicted that China would adopt communist ideals, at a time when such a thing was ideologically inconceivable. She is also said to have foreseen the partitioning of India into two separate states two years before the event, the assassination of Mahatma Ghandi and the surprise defeat of Winston Churchill in the post-war election of July 1945. She often gave specific dates well in advance and has frequently been proved correct to the very day, although she is by no means infallible. In fact, her failures reveal more about the nature of prophecy and prediction than do her successes.

# FAMOUS FAILURES

Despite her record for accuracy, Jeane Dixon has had her failures. Her most glaring error was to predict a major war for the 1980s, a decade comparatively free of conflicts that might be considered to have had significant global consequences. Other misses include her assurance that the Vietnam War would only last 90 days and that, in a period now past, China would use germ warfare against the United States and the Soviet Union would invade Iran and Israel. While she correctly predicted that the Shah of Iran would be overthrown and exiled, she was incorrect in dating the event to 1977 (he was deposed two years later) and wrong again in predicting his triumphant return. He died in exile. Several politicians whom she tipped for high office have long since disappeared from public life and into obscurity, from which it is inconceivable they will return.

It would appear that psychic energies are as much subject to ebb and flow as our physical and emotional energies, and can be restored or depleted, thus affecting judgement. It may be difficult for psychics to detect when their energy levels are low, and it is possible they may unconsciously deceive themselves in their interpretation of a vision, or in giving significance to something that is no more than a feeling, a 'hunch', just as we can deceive ourselves into feeling better – literally 'psyching ourselves up'– or talk ourselves into believing the worst. Psychics are human too!

# JEANE DIXON — A VISION OF THE ANTI-CHRIST

**High-society psychic Jeane Dixon's reputation for accuracy is such that her interpretations of her own visions are rarely questioned. Such is the case with her much publicized prediction foretelling the rise of a new religious leader towards the end of this century, a world leader opposed to Christianity, who will not be exposed as the Antichrist until 1999.**

A t dawn on 5 February 1962 Jeane Dixon awoke and crossed to her bedroom window to gaze out at the familiar Washington streets. But instead she was struck by a vision of a vast desert gilded by the rising sun. In the foreground stood an Egyptian pharaoh and his queen, whom Dixon instinctively recognized as Pharaoh Akhenaten and Queen Nefertiti. The royal couple were holding hands while Nefertiti cradled a new-born baby in her other arm. The baby appeared to be swaddled in rags, which was unusual for a royal child, and was then given to a crowd of strangers. Nefertiti then departed, stopping along the way to drink from a water jug. But as she stooped to drink she was murdered by an unseen assassin who stabbed her in the back with a dagger.

The scene then changed to reveal the child, now an adult, being surrounded by worshippers drawn from around the world. Before the vision faded she recalled experiencing an overwhelming feeling of 'perfect peace', a description which seems to contradict what she was later to claim (see box).

Mrs Dixon's initial interpretation of the images was that a child had just been born in Egypt to impoverished parents, a couple who were descendants of the royal couple Nefertiti and Akhenaten, and that throughout the 1980s and 1990s he would unite all races and religions in a new faith which she believed would be a new form of Christianity.

The most extraordinary aspect of the story is that she should put a definite and limited interpretation on such an

> **Could it be that Jeane Dixon did not have a presentiment of the future, but a revelation — which is the true meaning of prophecy?**

*In Mrs Dixon's vision Queen Nefertiti gave birth to a messiah who was later revealed as the Antichrist.*

ambiguous dream, especially bearing in mind the inclusion of the pre-Christian figures of Akhenaten and Nefertiti.

Akhenaten is believed to have been the originator of monotheism – the belief in one God – for which it is thought he was overthrown by an embittered Egyptian priesthood. Archaeological evidence suggests that he was exiled into the desert with a number of Hebrew slaves whom he converted to his new religion, which formed the basis of modern Judaism.

Could it be that Jeane Dixon did not in fact have a presentiment of the future, but rather a revelation – which is the true meaning of prophecy? A revelation could be accompanied by a feeling of 'perfect peace', which she claims to have experienced, and would hold an even greater significance than that which she had proclaimed.

An equally plausible explanation of the vision, which is surely no more fanciful than that which Mrs Dixon presumed to make, is that it was an insight into the universality of religion which she was denying due to her own rigid Catholicism – an insight for her own enlightenment and not intended for publication.

Jeane Dixon's critics complain that she assumes too much, arguing that her dogmatic Christianity imposes certain preconceptions and prejudices which prevent her impartial interpretation of her more symbolic visions. She herself, has admitted, 'I see symbols. They are always right, but I can misinterpret them.'

*Jeane Dixon believed that the Antichrist would be a descendant of Nefertiti and Akhenaten.*

## THE COUNTERFEIT CHRIST

Despite Mrs Dixon's initial insistence that her vision of Akhenaten and Nefertiti foretold the birth of a new messiah for the 1990s, a few years later she made a radical revision prompted by a second vision.

In the second vision she learnt that the child had been taken back to Egypt by his parents, where, in the mid-1970s, he would discover his true nature. Through the 1980s and 1990s he would establish a spurious new religion based on Christianity and Eastern philosophy, but which in fact would be a 'front' for the recruitment of a private army. By the mid-1990s he will control a worldwide media network with which he will corrupt the innocent before his true identity as the Antichrist is revealed in 1999. Then his followers will fall away, disillusioned and disappointed, and return like penitent prodigals to Christianity.

It is possible that one of the many false prophets expected to hijack the headlines on the eve of the millennium will fit Dixon's description.

*Egypt, the birth place of the Antichrist, according to Jeane Dixon.*

And there will be those who persist in the myth, pointing out the fact that on 4 February 1962, the day before her first vision, there had been a solar eclipse and an extraordinary conjunction of seven planets in the sign of Aquarius - a very important portent indeed.

# KARMOHAKSIS

**Few people have heard of the twentieth-century prophet Karmohaksis, who foretold the outbreak of AIDS, and fewer still of the events he predicted. The reason is simple: he broke the first rule of prophecy. He was so eager to be proved right that he gambled his reputation by giving precise dates for his vague visions and was consequently dismissed as a fake when the deadlines didn't match up with the disasters.**

*The mile-long memorial quilt laid before the US Capitol in October 1996 represented the 37,000 victims claimed by AIDS.*

n 1959 Italian booksellers were approached by the representatives of a publishing house based in Rome and urged to stock up with copies of a new book they were told would rival the *Centuries* of Nostradamus. The title of the book was *Le Primi Luce della Terza Era* ('The Dawn of the Third Era') by a new author who wished to be known only by his surname, Karmohaksis. No further details about the author were given, but his pronouncements were sufficiently dramatic to attract the attention of the national press and to fuel debate on the fate and future of the world.

Karmohaksis based his predictions on a premise he shared with the thirteenth-century prophet Joachim of Fiore, who had conceived the idea of history being divided into three distinct ages. The First Age Joachim described as the Age of the Father, which refers to the mosaic law of the Old Testament. The Second Age he called the Age of the Sun, under the influence of Jesus. The Third was the Age of the Holy Spirit, which he predicted would begin between 1200 and 1260 and would last until the Millennium. In spiritual terms they represented Fear, Faith and Freedom. However, unlike Joachim, Karmohaksis could not resist putting a date to the start of the spiritual millennium. In naming 2033 he had chosen a year significantly distant that he could not be discredited if it failed to materialize, and yet it would be close enough to capture public interest. After all, his readers would naturally be anxious about what the future held for their children and grandchildren who would be living at the time that the event predicted was due to come to pass.

Karmohaksis offered reassurance by describing the new world to come as a paradise where man and nature would coexist in perfect harmony. His readers' grandchildren would be the vanguard of a new race, but first there must be a new Flood to cleanse the world. Here the prophet's preoccupation with Biblical mythology corrupted his prophecies with preconceptions.

The first signs of the new age, he wrote, will be a series of natural disasters beginning in 1970 and lasting for fifteen years. So much for the start of a spiritual millennium! Cyclones, tidal waves, earthquakes and volcanic eruptions will leave large areas of the world's surface under water, including much of mainland Europe and the Sahara Desert. In fact, no such disasters took place during the period, although parts of Italy, Belgium and Holland were flooded in the early 1990s. Non-believers could be forgiven for saying that the law of averages, rather than the law of nature, was at work here. Such disasters were likely to happen sooner or later, especially given such a long timescale. But again, Karmohaksis made the error of being too specific. He named towns, cities and regions to be the worst affected only to be proved wrong by events. Further inaccuracies included the invention of spherical ships in the early 1970s, the death of the Pope in 1995, and the advent of universal brotherhood by 1985.

## NEW WORLD PEACE

Karmohaksis hit close to the mark though with his prediction of an incurable new disease being discovered at the end of the century, although he dated it to 1995 with the danger over by 1997. Coincidentally, after assertions that AIDS is incurable the possibility of a cure now seems likely with the first drugs becoming available in 1997.

As with most beliefs there are those who still do not accept that Karmohaksis could be wrong. They cite tenuous links between his description of a new world plague with the outbreak of AIDS, arguing that the prophet's facts were correct even if his dates were awry. The same could be said of his assertion that there would be riots in London and Paris, events which did actually take place, but in 1968, not in the early 1970s, as he had predicted. And did he not foresee the disarmament programme and the scaling down of conventional forces throughout Europe which followed the ending of the Cold War? Perhaps, but it could also be argued that if he had followed the prevailing trend in the 1950s of predicting a nuclear holocaust, few would have read his book.

**Let us hope the first sign of change will be the loss of our fear of the future.**

*Could Karmohaksis have foreseen the advent of the AIDS virus which infected this five-year-old girl and her mother?*

# ATLANTIS RISEN

In the midst of the destruction envisaged by Karmohaksis for the period preceding the Third Age, new lands will emerge from the sea, the first between Australia and New Zealand. The second land set to rise reveals the dubious sources of this prophet's predictions – it is Atlantis, which he claims will reappear in the Atlantic.

The legend of Atlantis, the 'lost continent', was central to the mythology of Madame Blavatsky, the Theosophists and the innumerable esoteric groups which can be considered their descendants. The perpetuation of the myth by Karmohaksis brings his credibility automatically into question. The accuracy of his prophecies must be balanced against a tendency to wishful thinking.

He states that the portion of Atlantis which will resurface will be about a quarter of the size of Australia. Its capital will be in ruins but much of its treasures will be found intact. The crystal dome which crowned the Temple of Poseidon will be found undamaged at the base of the seven brass pillars that had supported it and nearby will be found metals unknown to modern man.

The rediscovery of Atlantis, a continent destroyed by God as a judgement on its people, will be taken as a sign of what could happen to the rest of the world if man loses his humanity. But surely if man has not learned this from his own history, he will not learn it from legends.

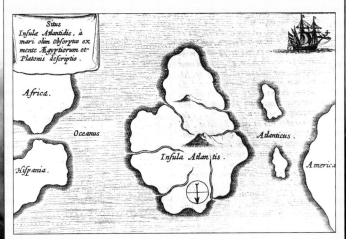

*The 'lost continent' of Atlantis is said to lie in the Atlantic.*

They further contend that his other prophecies, foretelling of an idyllic Third Age, is still in the process of coming to pass and that the so-called New Age movement is part of the gestation period which precedes it. The wheels of the universe, they assure us, grind exceedingly slowly. Changes on such a cosmic scale are rarely perceived by mere mortals. Such evolutionary developments are almost imperceptible to the mass of humanity for they happen outside our conception of time. That may well be, but as an argument it has long provided an all-too convenient refuge for false prophets and their credulous followers. If we are indeed heading towards a new age of enlightenment and heightened consciousness, let us hope the first sign of change will be the loss of our fear of the future.

# A QUESTION OF TIME

**In the 1930s the psychic researcher J. W. Dunne captured the public imagination with his theory that our dreams often contain precognitive visions, a phenomenon that he called 'dreaming true'. Dunne believed that if we made a note of our dreams immediately on waking we would find that many of them were previews of future events.**

*The playwright and novelist J.B. Priestley was fascinated by the possibility of serial time.*

Most of us are unaware of these fleeting glimpses into the future because they are obscured by the surreal imagery of the subconscious, and so are dismissed on waking by the conscious mind as being of no value. To eliminate this self-imposed censorship, Dunne proposed that we should all keep a Dream Journal for recording the details of our dreams which could then be compared with subsequent events.

The biggest problem would be in making a correct interpretation, as dream imagery is often symbolic and composed of distorted fragments (an idea which he borrowed from Freud).

To explain the problem, Dunne cited the example of a man who dreamt that he was being attacked by people who were throwing burning cigarettes at his face. Some days later the man was sprayed with sparks when the circular saw he was using struck a nail. The curious fact was that the future events Dunne recorded were often trivial and of no lasting significance for the people who dreamt them. Dunne's own dreams, however, were far more revealing.

On one occasion he dreamt of a volcanic eruption in which 4,000 people were killed. Some time later he learned that there had been an eruption, in Martinique, but a newspaper report claimed that as many as 40,000 people had lost their lives. The final death toll was somewhere between the two, a fact which convinced Dunne that what he had 'seen' in his dream was not the eruption itself but the newspaper report which he had misread, mistaking 40,000 dead for 4,000.

Dunne went on to formulate a theory of 'Serial Time' to explain the phenomena, a theory which stated that if time flows in one direction like a river, then there must be another form of time by which we can measure its speed, and another by which we measure this second form of time, and so on.

To explain the possibility of precognition, Dunne proposed another theory, that there are numerous levels of consciousness within each human being. The 'lowest' one

> We are only aware when we disengage our conscious mind and allow our intuitive self free rein.

would be aware only of this material world, while a higher Self would be able to peer over the physical barriers of matter to recall events in the past, or to look forward to the future.

The playwright J.B. Priestley took Dunne's theory of Serial Time a stage further, declaring that there are three tributaries, or dimensions, of time – 'everyday time' which passes by unobserved as we busy ourselves in mundane tasks; 'contemplative time' of which we are aware when we detach ourselves from the world through meditation and appear to lose our sense of time; and a third form which we are aware of only in moments of intense creativity. The latter, he believed, must be that in which the unconscious mind exists and which we are only aware of when we disengage our conscious mind and allow our intuitive self free rein.

*Priestley's most famous play,* Time and the Conways, *explores the effects of serial time on individuals.*

Priestley's fascination with the paradox of precognition led him to collate hundreds of cases, including one which seemed to indicate that premonitions are warnings from that third dimension – the subconscious.

He recorded the case of a mother who dreamt that she had left her baby by a river while she went to fetch some soap. When she returned the child had drowned. That summer, during a camping holiday, the mother took her child to a river and was about to leave it by the water's edge, intending to return to the tent for the soap, when she recognized the location. She grabbed the child and took it back to the tent with her, presumably saving its life.

*According to Priestley, when we are absorbed in mundane tasks we are in the dimension of 'everyday time'.*

# PARALLEL WORLDS

Dunne's theory of Serial Time led him to explore the possibility of there being serial, or parallel, universes, a concept many serious scientists have considered since. The theory is that every time each one of us makes a choice, the universe physically branches off on a new course while a duplicate takes the alternative route.

The contention is that the existence of parallel universes, each with the same inhabitants as our own, but with a different history, would explain how it is possible for previously reliable psychics to foresee other events which do not actually take place; the explanation being that the events have taken place, but in a replica universe, not in our own.

An argument against this idea is that while it is certainly possible for us to exist at different levels of consciousness simultane-ously, it would be physically and spiritually impossible for more than one version of ourselves and our universe to exist at the same point in time and space.

An altered state of consciousness, or heightened perception, attained by putting the ego or conscious mind to sleep, is the most likely explanation for precognition. Constructing an elaborate theory in which every individual decision we make creates a new replicate universe just to explain the inconsistency of inaccurate psychics is illogical, implausible, unscientific and plainly absurd.

Besides, time is not linear. Like the seasons it is cyclical, but not repetitive. Time is a man-made concept for marking the process of change as we perceive it, but to use it to measure the infinite is to limit our perception of a greater reality.

# THE PLANETS AND PREDICTIONS — THE GRAND CROSS

**Studying the effects of planetary influence on the earth was once thought to be the sole preserve of astrologers, but recently even eminent scientists have acknowledged that sun spots and certain planetary alignments can have catastrophic geological effects on our planet. Many now fear the effects that might be generated by a unique configuration of planets known as the Grand Cross, an event anticipated for 1999.**

In 1980 Professor Hideo Itokawa, a driving force behind Japan's rocket programme, appeared on Japanese television to announce that his calculations indicated the strong possibility of a global catastrophe before the end of the century. The professor's prediction was based on the fact that on 18 August 1999 the Sun and planets will assume the pattern of a Great Cross in the heavens, a rare event which could have cataclysmic consequences for life on earth. His pronouncement was given credence by the fact that scientists investigating the causes of major earthquakes and volcanic eruptions in the 1970s and 1980s had concluded that the marked increase in these upheavals over the

*Although the likelihood of a rogue asteriod colliding with the earth is very small, the possibility of a freak collision grows stronger every day. There are estimated to be over 40,000 of these minor planets orbiting the sun, only 4,000 of which have been identified.*

**Professor Hideo Itokowa indicated a strong possibility of a global catastophe before the end of the century.**

period and the accompanying climactic changes were indirectly related to increased sunspot activity and planetary alignments. Scientists Stephen Plagemann and John Gribbin had used their research into the relationship between planetary alignment and geological activity to predict that 1982 would see an increase in earthquakes due to all the planets (with the exception of the earth and moon) being to one side of the sun. Unprecedented earthquake activity that year appeared to prove their theory. Moreover, the increase in earthquakes during 1982 corresponded to a similar string of disasters in 1803, the last occasion when these planets were in the same position.

While the prospect of the formation of a Grand Cross in 1999 worries those who will monitor its geological influence, it is causing even greater concern among those astrologers who are inclined to attribute mystical significance to its appearance. These astrologers point out that the cross will appear in Taurus, Leo, Scorpio and Aquarius whose archaic symbols correspond with the four mythical beasts of the Apocalypse. Coincidentally, perhaps, these are also the four symbols depicted on the last card of the Tarot pack, which represents the world. This portent of doom, they claim, is emphasized by the fact that the conjunction will be preceded the week before by the last solar eclipse of the twentieth century and that the pattern will include the three maleficent planets Saturn, Uranus and Mars.

> **The prospect of a Grand Cross in 1999 is causing even greater concern among those astrologers who are inclined to attribute mystical significance to its appearance.**

Sceptics might consider the fact that the last rare planetary conjunction of occult significance, that of Neptune and Uranus in March 1993, coincided with severe snow storms and flooding across the United States, the worst for over 100 years. In naming Neptune, the God of Water, the ancients appear to have known the secrets of the stars. Astrologers will also have noted the significance of Uranus, whose presence is believed to determine the severity of these natural forces.

The bad news is that if we survive unscathed the effects of the Grand Cross, we can expect to be placed in the path of further peril with the appearance of the Great Conjunction scheduled to appear less than a year later. In May 2000 Pluto and the earth will be the only planets on their side of the sun, and the imbalance this produces could set off violent sunspot activity which could have potentially catastrophic consequences for humankind.

## THE CYCLE OF CULTURAL CHANGE

Astrologers believe that the Uranus-Neptune conjunction, which occurred in 1993, has initiated a cycle of cultural change to take us into the next millennium. Its significance can be gleaned from the fact that astrologers rate it second only to the Uranus-Pluto conjunction in Virgo which took place in 1965 and which initiated a spiritual awakening throughout the Western world.

The characteristics associated with Uranus are change, intuition and instinctive action, characteristics reflected in events occurring during the period of its influence. The planet itself was first noted in 1781, during the so-called Age of Revolution, and is said to govern technology - its discovery coinciding with the discovery of electricity. Its reappearance in the 1990s has coincided with the personal computer boom, the launch of satellite TV, and the introduction of the Internet and interactive multimedia.

The qualities of Neptune are the fluid qualities of imagination, emotion and idealism, but the planet also governs the development of chemistry, including drugs and alcohol. It is certainly true that since 1993 there have been an increasing number of dramatic medical breakthroughs, but conversely the problem of drug abuse has become more insidious and widespread to the point where it is undermining the structure of society.

Neptune's negative aspects can be seen in the proliferation of apocalyptic cults, institutionalized political corruption, mass misinformation, dissolution and nihilism which has marked the 1990s.

The conjunction of these strong, polarized planets promises a period of struggle for the soul of the human race. Intellect will struggle against emotion, religion against science, nihilism against spirituality. But, according to astrologers, the new millennium will offer a heaven-sent opportunity to reconcile these opposites.

*The number of computer users 'surfing' the World Wide Web has increased dramatically since 1989 – proof of a technological New Age as we move into the new Millenium.*

# RENNES-LE-CHÂTEAU — THE FALSE APOCALYPSE

**For over a century the small French village of R e n n e s - l e - Château is believed to have guarded a secret** that could shake the foundations of Western civilization. Clues said to be encoded in the surrounding countryside have inspired modern researchers to embark on an almost mythical quest which some believe may reveal a mystical message for mankind that can save us from the apocalypse to come.

*Poussin's 'The Shepherdess of Arcadia' which Van Buren, Andrews and Schellenbreger believed held the secret of Rennes-le-Château.*

**The secret might involve proof that Jesus did not die on the cross.**

The mystery of Rennes-le-Château began in 1885 when the Parish priest Abbé Berenger Saunier returned from a meeting with the Church fathers in Paris with sufficient funds to redecorate his impoverished provincial church in extravagant fashion. He even had enough money left over to build himself a lavish mansion and live in a style far beyond that which his meagre salary could sustain. It was said that he had discovered something of great value after decoding an ancient manuscript which had been found by chance in his church. There were rumours that he had uncovered the hidden wealth of the Knights Templar, whose plunder from the crusades has never been found. There was talk, too, of the lost treasure of the Cathars, a heretical Christian sect of the thirteenth century who were besieged at Montségur in Provence in 1244, but who are known to have smuggled something valuable out before their stronghold was overrun. Perhaps the Abbé might even have uncovered the Holy Grail, the chalice Jesus is said to have drunk from at the Last Supper? Whatever it was, he took the secret with him to the grave.

There was little more to add to the mystery than intense speculation and rumour until the publication in 1982 of *The Holy Blood and the Holy Grail*, a controversial best-seller in which the authors Henry Lincoln, Michael Baigent and

Richard Leigh suggested that the Abbé may have been paid for his silence rather than for sacred relics or treasure. Lincoln and his co-authors followed a complex trail of clues, the accumulation of which led them to conclude that the secret might involve proof that Jesus did not die on the cross, but had been revived by his disciples and smuggled out of Palestine. They also speculated that during the remainder of his life Jesus might even have fathered a child and that the proof of this lineage may have been encoded in the manuscript.

**If they are correct Christianity would be deprived of the founding myth of Christ's resurrection.**

If they are correct, Christianity would be deprived of the founding myth of Christ's resurrection along with the attendant beliefs in the Apocalypse, Armageddon, the Second Coming and the spiritual millennium.

In 1986 the mystery took on an even more fanciful dimension with the publication of *Refuge of the Apocalypse* by Elisabeth Van Buren. Her highly imaginative, but implausible, theory boiled down to a belief that the Abbé had discovered the location of the original Temple of Solomon in his own backyard, a temple built by 'Cosmic Intelligences' for use by descendants of a lost tribe of Israel! Van Buren maintained that the temple was a key to the Mysteries, a 'doorway into other dimensions', which contains a last-minute warning for mankind, namely that civilization will suffer an 'ordeal by fire' before its rebirth for the New Age. Her thesis hinges on clues she claims were encoded in the prophecies of Nostradamus, in the writings of Jules Verne and Rabelais and in paintings by Leonardo Da Vinci and Nicholas Poussin.

Ten years later, with concrete proof of these earlier theories still not uncovered, underwater archaeologist Richard Andrews and civil engineer Paul Schellenberger set out to follow an even more elaborate trail which they described in detail in their book *The Tomb of God*. They were excited by what appeared to be a convincing link

*The Church of Rennes-le-Château, where the Abbé is said to have unearthed a remarkable secret.*

between occult geometrical patterns, which they claim to have found in the Da Vinci and Poussin paintings, and actual locations in the region of Rennes-le-Château. Schellenberger had convinced Andrews that he had located the site of significant topographical clues by super-imposing the geometrical patterns found in the paintings over a map of the area. The pair then set out to prove their theory. This appeared to be confirmed by a profusion of cryptograms, riddles, anagrams and symbols found on grave stones, landmarks and in a photocopy of the legendary manuscript.

The trail eventually led them to a mountain range within sight of Rennes-le-Château where, they believe, is located the tomb of Jesus.

## THE FAKE AND THE FACTS

The labyrinthine trail plotted with such esoteric enthusiasm by Elisabeth Van Buren and later, more clinically, by Andrews and Schellenberger, can be traced back to clues they each claimed to have detected in the paintings of Poussin and Da Vinci .

They believed that prints of the paintings had been bought from the Louvre by the Abbé for closer study after he had decoded references to them in the manuscript. However, recent research has revealed that the Louvre have no record of the Abbé having bought the prints and, more significantly, that the manuscript at the heart

of the mystery is allegedly a fake. A French journalist has since produced the original document which is autographed by one of the two hoaxers who was intent on spoiling the joke after the pair had fallen out over money.

Perhaps it is no surprise that Andrews and Schellenberger maintain the validity of their conclusions despite these recent revelations. They appear to have made the same error as many misguided prophets in that they set out to prove a preconceived idea because it was more appealing than the facts.

# THE LAWS OF PROPHECY

**In his comprehensive, and rather controversial study of prophecy and predictions,** *The Armageddon Script,* **author Peter Lemesurier identifies what he considers to be the Seven Laws of Prophecy. These, he suggests, govern predictions and their fulfilment - predictions which we, consciously or unconsciously, endeavour to fulfil and which condition our actions in the present.**

The First Law, that of Surprise Fulfilment, encapsulates the fact that the most likely outcome is the one which nobody has anticipated; a conclusion which is inconsistent with the vast number of accurate predictions recorded elsewhere in this book!

Lemesurier's argument is that the circumstances to which a prophecy refers can be known only to the prophet who uttered it. Not being able to share the vision of the prophet denies a vital clue to those who attempt to interpret it. Furthermore, the way in which a prophecy is expressed, and the context in which it was made, make an accurate interpretation by anyone else, particularly someone from another culture and another age, almost impossible.

Good examples of this are the innumerable pronouncements concerning the Second Coming and the End of the World which have been based on spurious interpretations of the Bible. The fact is that to date every single would-be prophet rash enough to put a date to either event prior to the present has been proved wrong. Furthermore, if and when either event takes place, Lemesurier argues that it will take a form no fundamentalist could foresee.

It is also a serious mistake, he says, to accept the prophecies of a symbolist such as Nostradamus at face value. Many of the seer's pronouncements offer no date for the events they describe and are open to a number of equally plausible interpretations which cannot all be correct. Lemesurier's contention is that they require an interpreter of considerable intuitive and intellectual ability. In short, he or she must be a prophet of equal stature otherwise the Second Law will be invoked, the Law of Thwarted Expectation. This states that the most obvious interpretation of a prophecy by a person of lesser talents is likely to be the wrong one.

It may seem obvious to the sceptic, but Lemesurier's Third Law identifies the influence of rigorous religious and nationalist beliefs as being highly prejudicial to the credibility of the would-be prophet. His Third Law, of Prejudicial Interference, states that preconceptions and predictions do not mix.

He identifies numerous prophets from St Malachy to Jeane Dixon who, he claims, superimposed their preconceptions on their own predictions. They wanted to

*Would-be prophets like Jeane Dixon foresaw China as the greatest threat to the West, but recent pro-democracy demonstrations may succeed in overthrowing the regime and eventually removing that threat. If so, it will illustrate Lemesurier's First Law of prophecy - that of Surprise Fulfilment.*

## THE PROPHECIES OF MOSES

To illustrate his Fourth Law of Prophecy, that of Self-fulfilment, Lemesurier cites the example of the prophecies of Moses, which predicted that the Israelites would break their covenant with God and be driven from their land. Lemesurier's argument is that, having been forewarned that they would live less than perfect lives, the Israelites were largely unwilling to defend themselves when they were overrun and enslaved by a succession of invaders. They saw the hand of Divine retribution in all that befell them, the will of God rather than the wilfulness of their persecutors. They considered that it was their destiny to be driven out and suffer through the centuries and so many of them accepted it without resistance. What they believed would happen to them, did happen.

Ironically, recent research reinforces the suspicion that these prophecies were attributed to Moses 900 years after his death by Hebrew scribes whose intention had been to reaffirm their religious laws and warn the people of the consequences of disobeying them.

*The prophecies of Moses foreseeing the Israelites' flight from Egypt illustrates the Fourth Law.*

believe in the Second Coming of Jesus Christ and his Millennial Kingdom and they also needed to believe in an Antichrist because his existence would provide a convenient and simple explanation of the presence and purpose of evil in the world. According to Lemesurier, Dixon also allowed her pride in the American way of life to reinforce her preconceived ideas of good and evil, with the Communist system condemned as the work of the Devil.

The Fourth Law is that of Self-fulfilment which is often demonstrated in a mundane form such as personal goal-setting. If someone does not believe that they will succeed, they undermine their effort by a lack of willpower and are destined to fail.

The Fifth Law, that of Diminishing Accuracy, states that the accuracy of a prophecy decreases as the square of the time to its fulfilment. In essence this means that so long as a prophet makes predictions within his own lifetime he is more likely to

be proven accurate, because he is able to draw considered conclusions from facts and circumstances he is familiar with. He is also more likely to foresee the obvious consequences of an action which in all probability will happen in the near future. But the further he predicts events from his own time the less accurate he is likely to be, because the world will have changed beyond his wildest imagining.

**The further ahead a prophet predicts events the less accurate he is likely to be.**

The penultimate Law, the Law of Prophetic Foreshortening, states that clairvoyance foreshortens the future. In other words, psychic foresight does not necessarily lead to greater insight, as a vision invariably offers only a close-up snapshot of the future rather than a wide-angle full length preview. Lemesurier likens it to someone trying to map the heavens by peering up a chimney. What we see in that portion of the sky cannot tell us about the cosmos.

The last identifiable Law is that of Non-Existent Impossibility which simply reminds us that if it can happen, it will; if it can't happen, it might.

*The First Law implies that only a prophet of equal ability to Nostradamus could accurately interpret his predictions.*

# GURUS AND PROPHETS OF THE NEW AGE

M uch of our unease concerning science and technology stems from the lurid speculations of the pulp science fiction magazines and movies which exploited the post-atomic Cold War paranoia prevalent in the 1950s. But as science fiction rapidly becomes science fact, we are beginning to lose our anxieties and with them the need for reassurance from would-be prophets, be they sacred, secular or scientific.

Already we are becoming better informed of the principles, if not the details, involved in creating the new world to come. Unfortunately, the pace of progress and the prospect of the unknown, represented by the new millennium, has made many people insecure.

According to the gurus and prophets of the New Age, this understandable, though irrational, anxiety has fanned the flames of religious fundamentalism which threatens to impede the spiritual evolution of humanity into the next millennium.

Those who are so eager for the End of the World often cite the words of Jesus of Nazareth as a warning of specific events which will afflict us at the End of Days: 'And ye shall hear of wars and rumours of wars; see that ye be not troubled; for all these things must come to pass, but the end is not yet. For nation shall rise against nation, and kingdom against kingdom; and there shall be famines, and pestilence and earthquakes in divers places.'

But is it not more likely that Jesus was condemning those of us who put our faith in false prophets and predictions? After all, in doing so we are entrusting our future to fate, or the whims of a capricious father-creator, rather than accepting our share of responsibility for the state of the world.

The only effective way to assuage our fear of the unknown is to accept the fact that 'these things must come to pass' and measure our success by how we are able to cope with them.

# VISIONS OF THE FUTURE

**Imagination is the key to true prophecy. And when an imaginative mind is focused by the intellect its prophecies are likely to prove more accurate than those of the most celebrated psychic. Such is certainly true in the case of the scientific visionaries Leonardo Da Vinci and Roger Bacon.**

Although he was not an inventor himself, the English Franciscan monk and alchemist Roger Bacon (c. 1214-1292) had a grasp of mechanical principles and a fascination with natural phenomena which combined with a breadth of imagination led him to predict some of the most significant inventions of the twentieth century. He foresaw the invention of aeroplanes, motor cars, tanks, and the laser, although he appeared to limit their use to warfare.

He wrote of 'bridges across rivers without piers or other supports ... burning glasses which operate at any distance we can choose, so that anything hostile to the commonwealth may be burnt - a castle, or army, or city, or anything; and the flying machine, and a navigating machine by which one man may guide a ship full of armed men with incredible speed; and scythe-bearing cars which full of armed men race along with wondrous machinery without horses to draw them, and break down, or cut through all obstacles'.

He also anticipated the development of the underwater diving suit, poison gas and optical lenses, while through his alchemical experiments he became one of the first Europeans to appreciate the potential of gunpowder.

His voracious appetite for knowledge was combined with a determination to prove the truth of every theory for himself. He was known to have a healthy distaste for scholars who relied exclusively on second-hand sources for their knowledge. Few academics at the time even had a working knowledge of ancient languages and so relied upon dubiously translated texts, whereas Bacon was versed in Greek, Hebrew and Arabic.

*Roger Bacon's vision of a flying machine was formed by his observation of birds and insects. Without the intellect and imagination of such visionaries, our modern world might not have taken the shape it has.*

He defied the self-appointed authorities of his time and was silenced by the Church for the 'novelty' of his writings, spending most of his adult life in enforced confinement in various monasteries and prisons, but he was to triumph over their ignorance.

As with Da Vinci, he was one of the few true visionaries whose writings actually inspired other men to action, to gauge the practicalities of his 'inventions' and thus fulfil his predictions. It was Bacon's writings which are said to have inspired Christopher Columbus to embark on a voyage that was to lead to the discovery of America.

> **Da Vinci considered it his duty in life to exercise his considerable intellect and imagination.**

Another influential English thinker was the politician, poet and philosopher Sir Francis Bacon (1561-1626), who, although no relation to Roger Bacon, almost matched his fellow countryman for visionary power.

In his philosophical fable *The New Atlantis* Sir Francis detailed the discovery of a new continent whose inhabitants are a community of scholars. His description of their multidisciplinary laboratory, the House of Solomon, anticipates the establishment of research laboratories by several hundred years.

Inside these laboratories, machinery – which Bacon called 'engines of motion' – are designed and tested. These machines would not become a fact for

*Da Vinci's designs were annotated with notes to prove that they were practical and based on sound scientific principles.*

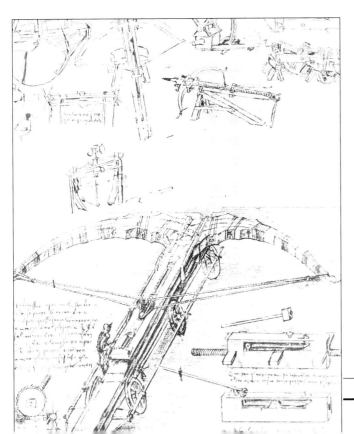

# THE GREAT DESIGNER

Leonardo Da Vinci (1452-1519) considered it his duty in life to exercise his considerable intellect and imagination maintaining that, 'Iron rusts from disuse, stagnant water loses its purity, and in cold weather becomes frozen; even so does inaction sap the vigors of the mind.'

His inventions, sketched in great detail and annotated to prove that the principles were sound, were the products of foresight rather than future-sight, but many were to prove both practical and indispensable in the future.

*Leonardo Da Vinci .*

He devised a prototype parachute ('a tent of linen'), a muscle-powered helicopter with speedometer and navigation devices, and a wheel jack which is almost identical to that manufactured for vehicles today.

For an Italian duke threatened by a belligerent neighbour, he supplied designs for a tank made of wood with sloping sides to deflect cannon balls which he called a 'mole'. It would be armed with cannon to scatter the enemy and noise devices to frighten their horses.

Other military devices included metal artillery shells and a breech-loading ten-barrel machine-gun with screw elevation, which would be key features of the Gatling gun manufactured 300 years later.

another two hundred years. Bacon even anticipated that the development of such machines for manufacturing purposes would eventually lead to a dependence on mass production.

From the study of sound, light and colour would come new inventions including one for transmitting sound 'over great distance through tubes', which sounds suspiciously like the telephone, and another which hints at the laser.

His method for distilling salt water into fresh water and his advocacy of hybrid agriculture and multi-crop gardens were actually put into practice in the 1950s and 1960s by the Israelis, whose vital trade in this area would not otherwise have thrived.

Bacon even devised a method for refrigerating food using ice, but he spent so much time in the company of frozen chickens that he caught a chill and died soon afterwards from pneumonia.

Without visionaries such as the Bacons and Da Vinci, our modern world may not have taken the form it has. Likewise, without technical expertise such inventions remain only an idea, a vision, a prediction waiting to be fulfiled.

# VISIONS OF THE FUTURE – THINGS TO COME

**It is the general view of researchers into precognition and the occult that artists and writers possess more highly developed psychic faculties than the average person. Certainly many authors of science fiction have proven remarkably farsighted, often anticipating technological developments greatly in advance of their own time. But are their prophecies to be taken as seriously as those made by psychics who claim paranormal perception?**

*Early science fiction writers imagined other planets in highly fanciful terms, but their writings were often proved accurate in principle and were an inspiration to the pioneers of space travel.*

Both the French writer Jules Verne (1828-1905) and his English contemporary H.G. Wells (1866-1946) treated space travel as a fanciful adventure, embroidering their whimsical tales with the genteel charm of the period, but nevertheless left many of their readers convinced of the possibility of space exploration.

In *From The Earth To The Moon* (1865) Verne launched his cylindrical craft from a huge gun barrel as if it was an artillery shell, but he was not so far out in his incidental detail, accurately predicting not only the journey time, escape velocity, crew capacity and principles of re-entry, but also the location of the launch site for the first manned moon landing. He named Tampa, Florida, which is only 123 miles from NASA's launch site at Cape Kennedy. He was even closer to the mark in stating that the journey time would be 97 hours 13 minutes and 20 seconds. In 1969 Apollo XI reached the moon in 97 hours 39 minutes and 17 seconds.

The pioneers of Verne's fantasy called their craft 'Columbiad' which is uncannily close to that of the Apollo XI module - Columbia. Both craft were cylinder-shaped and manned by a crew of three, their re-entry controlled by rockets and their splashdown occurring in the Pacific.

Although the flight was pure fantasy, Verne's choice of aluminium for the outer shell of the spacecraft was an inspired one. In 1901 it convinced the first aircraft manufacturers to build the frames of their airships from what had previously been considered too precious a metal for industrial use. And by 1917 the second generation of fighter aircraft were also being constructed of aluminium.

> **Verne described buildings buzzing with clerks 'bent over their computers'!**

In 1875, at the height of his fame, Verne presumed to make the following predictions in a lecture entitled 'In the 29th Century'. He described the major cities of the distant future as having up to 10 million inhabitants (a fair estimate of the population of the average city of the 1990s) with streets 100 yards wide and lined by skyscrapers. These buildings will be kept at an 'equable temperature' by a form of air-conditioning and will be buzzing with clerks 'bent over their computers'!

Evidently even a writer of Verne's imagination could not conceive of the pace of change which made possible the developments he had predicted for the twenty-ninth century coming into existence less than one hundred years after his death.

H.G. Wells was more of an idealist than Verne, and was intensely aware of the dangers as well as the potential of science. He once noted that although there were numerous professors of history there was not a single Professor of Foresight in the world who would consider the consequences of our present actions on the future. It is likely that he put himself in that role as he foresaw the advent of television, genetic engineering, tanks, aerial warfare and the atom bomb in futuristic fables such as *The Time Machine*, *When The Sleeper Wakes*, *The War In The Air*, *The First Men In The Moon* and *The Shape of Things To Come*.

But, being an idealist, he was more concerned with the future welfare of mankind, which he could not foresee benefiting in any way other than in material comfort and convenience from the technological innovations of the future.

He died despairing that mankind was not competent to control the forces it was so eager to unleash.

## PUMPHINS AND PREDICTIONS

Although Jules Verne and H.G. Wells are regarded as the fathers of modern science fiction, they were pre-empted in predicting the problems of space travel by the seventeenth-century German astronomer and astrologer Johannes Keppler.

In a novel entitled *Somnium* (1634) Keppler struggled with the practicalities of gravitational pull, weightlessness and the lack of oxygen in space three hundred years before they were of concern to the pioneers of the NASA space programme.

As part of his duties as court astronomer in Graz Keppler was responsible for compiling an annual astrological almanac, although in principle he was against making predictions. He considered himself to be a man of science, making his prophecies under protest and yet, he proved to be uncommonly accurate.

In his first almanac he correctly predicted the invasion of Austria by the Ottoman Turks in 1594 and he accurately forecast bitterly cold weather for that winter in which hundreds of people died. When pressed to explain his ability he remarked: '[The heavens] act on [a man] during his life in the manner of the loops which a peasant ties at random around the pumpkins in his field; they do not cause the pumpkin to grow, but they determine its shape ...'

*Jules Verne, regarded by many as the father of science fiction.*

*Jules Verne was uncannily accurate in predicting the incidental detail of man's first flight to the moon.*

# BRAVE NEW WORLD

**Just as the ancients formed their expectations of the future from their own mythology and later generations were influenced by Biblical promises of a millennial Eden, so twentieth-century society has largely formulated its hopes and fears from the prophets of popular culture - the science fiction writers and filmmakers.**

With the ending of the Cold War and the threat of global nuclear annihilation apparently receding, so our uncertainty and suspicion of science is being replaced by a genuine concern for the price we and the planet are being forced to pay for progress. These concerns, human, ecological and technological, have found their most eloquent expression in the prophecies of the more serious SF writers of the post-war period whose visions of life in the next millennium are far more credible than the flights of fancy dreamt up by their pre-war predecessors. Many are based on sound scientific reasoning and rational reactions to a challenging future and are therefore more likely to be proved accurate because they put probability above prediction.

Unlike the psychic visionaries who proclaim their vision of the future as fact, the SF prophets present a possible future for our appraisal in which our aspirations and absurdities are reflected and intensified. The more pessimistic among them envisage an apocalyptic scenario to match any foreseen by their evangelistic predecessors if we continue to ignore the arrogant, conceited devil within our own heads. It will be a living hell of our own making, a high-tech, de-humanizing global metropolis, with civilization ultimately degenerating into anarchy through the pressures of overpopulation, dwindling resources and state control.

But the majority affirm that the unknown, whether it be our own future or the 'final frontier' of outer space, should be regarded as friendly and that our pioneering spirit and restless curiosity will ensure we determine our own destiny. The next millennium may even witness the human race, the Created, assuming the role of Creator, if we can master the mysteries of life, degeneration, disease and death – mysteries which we are only now beginning to understand.

Already aspects of Aldous Huxley's *Brave New World* are becoming a reality in the 1990s, but his nightmarish vision of a state-controlled, genetically-engineered society has hopefully forewarned us of the potential dangers, so that instead we can develop genetics towards personal and planetary regeneration.

*The DNA molecule, which holds the key to genetic engineering and many medical advances in the future.*

> Many SF prophecies are based on sound scientific reasoning and are therefore more likely to be proved accurate because they put probability above prediction.

If we are to fulfil the promise of the SF prophets, those who predict continuing technological innovation, it must be on condition that we have matured to a level where we accept the responsibilities that go with it.

And, indeed, the more optimistic writers echo the message of the mystics and the New Age gurus in that the growth and development of the individual will be mirrored in the evolutionary pattern of the human race. We are currently going through the trials of adolescence, but with the new millennium will come maturity. The writer Robert A. Heinlein expects that the transition to the next millennium will be characterized by 'Civil disorder, followed by the end of human adolescence and [the] beginning of [the] first mature culture.'

Throughout the ages prophets have proclaimed the coming of a new world, whether it is a new Eden or a post-apocalyptic wasteland. But their predictions are invariably based on their dubious intuition and overactive imaginations. The imaginative writer who sets his tale in the future fulfils a more valuable function by describing how we will react when we get there and how we will make the best of what we find.

The SF writer is a modern prophet inviting us to consider the same moral choices faced by characters in the bible, fables and mythology. It is no coincidence that so many SF tales predict an apocalypse followed by the discovery of a new Eden. Forearmed and forewarned we can predict our own future with confidence and through the foresight which fiction offers we can also get a fresh perspective on the human condition.

*The creator of the cult TV series* Star Trek *devised several significant scientific devices which have since become reality.*

## THE SCIENCE OF STAR TREK

In their enthusiasm to 'boldly go where no man has gone before' the producers of the TV series *Star Trek* were forced to resolve technical problems of futuristic complexity. The question is that in doing so, did they preempt the technology which is now a part of our daily lives, or did their show act as an inspiration to the real innovators who would later produce these devices?

In the case of the hypospray and the mobile phone it was definitely a case of life imitating art. The hypospray, a pressurized hypodermic drug injector which *Star Trek*'s scriptwriters dreamt up in the 1960s, became a medical reality in the 1990s, about the same time as the mobile phone made its appearance – apparently inspired by the cordless communicators used by Captain Kirk and his crew.

The first spin-off series *Star Trek – The Next Generation* made extensive use of 3D holographic computer-generated X-ray Imaging in scenes showing the interior of the USS *Enterprise*, and the medical examinations of its crew members. Such technology was only theoretical at the time, but has since become a feature of advanced key-hole surgery in the USA.

Incredibly, NASA scientists have recently confirmed that they now have a satellite communications complex which functions exactly like the control system on the bridge of the USS *Enterprise* and that they regard the series as a 'magnification' of what they hope to do by the twenty-third century. But whether the imagination of the show's scriptwriters regarding Warp drives and Wormholes will be matched by the inventiveness of twenty-third century scientists will depend on whether our best brains can overcome the limiting laws of physics.

# OSHO – GURU OF THE NEW AGE ?

**Bhagwan Shree Rajneesh (1931-90), more widely known as Osho, has been alternately praised by his followers as 'the greatest spiritual teacher of the twentieth century' and condemned by his critics as 'the most dangerous man since Jesus Christ'.**

The personality cult which developed around this apparently astute, well-educated Indian with a penchant for collecting Rolls Royce motor cars has not dissolved with his death. Thousands of ardent disciples continue to be drawn every year to the commune he established in Poona, India, a landscaped utopia described as a 'spiritual Disneyland for disaffected First World yuppies'. His teachings continue to attract new converts who have become disillusioned with orthodox religion and are impressed by the 600 books published by the worldwide organization dedicated to recording and promoting his discourses. Whatever anxieties these devotees may have regarding his image and reputation as a 'giggling guru', few fail to be impressed by his ability to condense the convoluted teachings of the Eastern mystics whilst salvaging the good sense from the doctrines of the Western religions.

*Osho predicted the end of Communism in Europe almost a year before the fall of the Berlin Wall.*

Osho's years as a philosophy student at the University of Jabalpur had given him a thorough grounding in the doctrines of the world's major religions, which he later reinterpreted for a new generation. His disciples and his detractors still disagree about his motives, but there can be no doubt that he was shrewdly aware that there was a new disaffected generation in the 1980s lacking the ideals of their hippie predecessors and impatient for spiritual enlightenment.

Many were captivated by Osho's erudition, charm and impish good humour. Others, no doubt, were attracted by his apparent obsession with sex and what they interpreted as his belief in sex being a path to super-consciousness. 'Sex is man's most vibrant energy, but it should not be an end unto itself: sex should lead man to his soul.'

## SEXUAL INDISCRETIONS

Such comments not surprisingly led to him being banned from twenty-one countries and condemned by religious leaders as the head of an insidious cult. Rumours of sexual indiscretions between the guru and female neophytes eventually led to his deportation from the United States in 1985 and were followed by stories of an attempted coup by warring factions within the organization, and even of an assassination attempt on the Master and his doctor. Osho denied all attempts by his followers to compare his 'persecution' with that of any previous messiah, claiming instead that he was the first manifestation of the new man he dubbed 'Zorba the Buddha' – a mix of the gregarious Greek fictional character Zorba and the enlightened Buddha.

**'Sex should lead man to his soul.'**

*Osho saw himself as the forerunner of enlightened human beings.*

Osho had assumed the mantle of a New Age prophet after rejecting the insular academic world at the age of thirty-two in order to tour India proclaiming his vision of a New Age. He once declared:

'The new man is not a hope: you are already pregnant with it. My work is just to make you aware that the new man has already arrived. My work is to help you to recognize and respect him.'

But, according to Osho, this evolutionary step will require enormous energy and the results will be more dramatic than the physical stages which have marked our evolution to date.

'From fish to man there has been evolution. But from man to a Buddha, from man to a Christ, from man to a Kabir [the Indian mystic], it is not evolution it is revolution.'

The New Age, he predicted, will offer us the chance to free ourselves from political and religious slavery and rediscover the simplicity and innocence of the spirit. Once we are centred in ourselves there will be no need for institutionalized religion.

'One day we are going to attain a society which will be harmonious, which will be far better than all the ideas that utopians have been producing for thousands of years. The reality will be far more beautiful.'

## OSHO'S PREDICTIONS

In 1988, a year before the fall of Communism in Russia, Osho gave an interview to a Soviet film crew in which he predicted the imminent disintegration of the Soviet Union as a direct result of Mikhail Gorbachev's reforms. Few outside the Soviet system could have foreseen such a momentous event. At the time there was little indication of growing dissent among the mass of the Russian people, while the fall of the Berlin Wall and the first cracks in the Communist enclave were still eleven months in the future. In an effort to discredit him the Soviet press dismissed Osho as a 'front' for the US Central Intelligence Agency, while the American authorities, it is claimed, did their best to undermine his credibility as a spiritual leader following his prediction that the United States would also break up in the near future!

But Osho was not a compulsive prophet of doom, rather a prophet in the tradition of the New Testament charismatics. He did not make a habit of producing headline-grabbing predictions, but intuitively foresaw the consequences of our ingrained attitudes and actions, which is another element of the prophetic gift.

He predicted that in the coming millennium the doctrines and dogmas of Western orthodox, institutionalized religion would be superseded by the intuitive understanding and simple devotion of the East. For Osho, Zen Buddhism was the one 'true' religion.

'As far as I can see, Zen is going to be paving the path for the new man to come, and for the new humanity to emerge ... Zen is a way of dissolving philosophical problems, not of solving them. It is a way of getting rid of philosophy, because philosophy is a sort of neurosis ... The greatest thing that Zen has brought into the world is freedom from oneself.'

*Osho predicted that the Soviet Union would disintegrate as a result of Gorbachev's reforms.*

# DAVID ICKE — THE GREEN PROPHET

**David Icke's image as a controversial media prophet threatens to obscure the very serious message he feels compelled to share with the world. He claims to be a channel for highly evolved spiritual beings whose upbeat prophecies for humanity's evolution are balanced by warnings of what might shortly befall us if we ignore them.**

When Icke, a former professional footballer, TV presenter and Green politician, visited the renowned medium and healer Betty Shine in March 1990, he was stunned to discover that not only had all the events in his life so far been preordained by spiritual guides, but that his 'mission' in this life was to be a channel for their message.

Icke's spiritual guides told him that, 'one man cannot change the world, but one man can communicate the message that can change the world'. He was convinced that he was dealing with the truth and that he would help to bring about a 'spiritual revolution', becoming a 'cosmic parent' to the planet and humanity.

Ever since he had been forced to give up a promising football career because of severe rheumatoid arthritis, and then drifted effortlessly into the dream careers of politics and television, Icke had suspected that a higher intelligence was guiding his life. Even his initial contact with Betty Shine had been the result of an irresistible compulsion to browse among the paperbacks at a railway station where he was inexplicably drawn to one of her books, although he had never heard of her before. Now, on meeting her and experiencing the energy which was to awaken his own latent psychic abilities,

> He was convinced that he was becoming a 'cosmic parent' to the planet.

*The earthquake which struck the Japanese city of Kobe in January 1995 was predicted by Icke's spirit guide in 1990.*

*David Icke proclaims 'the message that can change the world'.*

these feelings were confirmed. Over the next weeks and months, by means of mediums and sensitives, Icke learnt that a great transformation of the human race is drawing close and that it is urgent and essential for our evolution that we prepare ourselves for the challenges it will present us with.

These new energies and vibrations, which he calls Truth Vibrations, began filtering through in the mid-1960s and will quicken and intensify in the late 1990s, culminating in a universal transformation as we enter the new millennium.

To assimilate this energy of transformation effectively, Icke's guides say we must let go of our preconceptions about life and death. We have to make a great leap in consciousness if we are to see the greater reality and our true place and purpose in the universe. Icke claims that humanity is already dividing into those who are tuned in to these vibrations and are evolving as predicted and those whose senses are dulled to their influence through a preoccupation with materialism. It seems that the most serious threat we face is from our own fear; fear of life, fear of death and fear of the future.

# THE PROPHECIES OF WANG YEE LEE

The first spirit guide to make contact with David Icke through the agency of medium and healer Betty Shine was Chinaman Wang Yee Lee. In Betty's vision Lee appeared dressed in the robes of a mandarin, but gave no information about himself other than that his last incarnation had been in the thirteenth century. Icke was later able to confirm that the description which Betty had given him of Lee's robes matched those of the period. Lee's purpose in appearing that day was to make the following predictions concerning Icke's career and the future of mankind.

Lee warned that the inner earth is being destabilized by the plundering of oil from the seabed. Consequently there would have to be destructive incidents to serve as a warning against this abuse of the environment. The earth would shortly be shaken by earthquakes in places where they had not previously been experienced. (And, indeed, four days after Lee made this prediction an earthquake measuring 4.9 on the Richter scale hit a large area along the Welsh-English border.) Lee described how, in the longer term, the earth's centre will shift and the position of the Poles will be altered with the

sea reclaiming land to prove that its spirits must be respected.

As for Britain, it will experience a cultural revolution in the mid-1990s - a prophecy which could be said to have come true if we accept that financial recessions, attendant poverty and a disturbing increase in crime leads to soul-searching and eventual social renewal. Spiritual transformation does not necessarily manifest as a millennial idyll, but can be seen as the emergence of a stronger society which has come to terms with its own demons.

By the year 2010 Lee promised that there will be a new form of aeroplane and that travel itself will undergo a revolution. Time, he said, would be meaningless with people whisked from one location to another at the speed of thought.

In conclusion Lee explained that Icke had been singled out as a healer of the earth because of his courage, although he was still a child in terms of spiritual development. During the course of Icke's campaign to increase spiritual and planetary awareness, he would encounter stiff opposition, but he would be guided and assisted in his work by higher beings.

# ICKE'S JOURNEY

**David Icke had been told that his prophecies would be spiritually inspired and that he would be drawn to sources of knowledge which would help his mission. Time after time he felt himself drawn to material which either confirmed what he had intuitively felt, or led him on to the next revelation.**

*Earthquakes and natural disasters are apparently warnings against abuse of the planet.*

One such book was entitled *We Are The Earthquake Generation* by American scientist Jeffrey Goodman. It was a comparative study of American psychics who were noted for their unerringly accurate predictions. Goodman, who was open minded on the subject, approached each of the psychics independently and asked what they predicted for the years immediately preceding the millennium. Astonishingly, they all concurred in their forecasts. There would be dramatic geological upheavals towards the year 2000 AD. Moreover, they each fleshed out their forecasts with detail that suggested that in their receptive trance-like states they had a grasp of advanced geological principles which they did not possess in their normal waking state.

What fascinated Icke, however, was not so much the detail but the basic principle behind the predictions which seemed to strengthen his suspicion that nature would strike back if man continued to flout Universal Laws by abusing and exploiting the planet.

These portents of natural disasters for the late 1990s and beyond were later 'confirmed' by various spirit guides Icke encountered through his psychic contacts. These beings explained that there were changes occurring at the earth's core which will initially manifest as volcanic eruptions in the east before triggering an entire earthquake cycle with attendant floods around the world. Our actions on earth, it seems, have upset the natural balance of life and the ripples are being felt not only in the physical universe, but also on the astral plane. Through our obsession with materialism, we have literally lost our old 'magic', our psychic sixth sense which made us sensitive to our environment and other forms of life, but we are destined to regain it. In the meantime, the task and responsibility of the evolved beings who watch over us is to redress the balance and harmonize the earth.

Already some of the catastrophic events foretold have been averted as a result of an increase in human awareness of the dangers of continuing on the present self-centred course. There is still time, Icke believes, to avert other predicted disasters if those people who are responsible for environmental destruction would wake up to the dire consequences of their actions.

**'Nature will strike back if man continues to flout Universal Laws.'**

Part of the coming transformation, he believes, will involve more of us taking such responsibility seriously and acting accordingly. In effect, we must expand our mental horizons to give ourselves a new perception of the universe.

Our concept of time is one example which illustrates our limited understanding of the totality of existence. Beyond the confines of the material world, Past, Present and Future are non-existent. There is only Being and Non-being. Time is a human concept which we devised to make ourselves feel secure and for the practical purposes of comparative measurement and orientation. Consequently, spirit guides existing outside our world are unable to give specific dates for the coming changes, and can only intimate that such developments are planned and that they involve a radical reappraisal of our current perception of reality.

*Icke's prophecies are the result of the knowledge he has been given by his spirit guides.*

# PREDICTIONS & PREDICTABILITY

As a prophet Icke is particularly interesting because he has grasped the fact that the pattern of the future is ever-changing in relation to actions we take and decisions we make in the present. In essence, the future is determined by the present.

The reason why predictions made by genuine psychics are usually borne out by events is simply because we usually act in a predictable way. Many psychics, for example, have foreseen the outbreak of wars because the protagonists acted according to their natures. Likewise, an aggressor invariably draws a totally predictable response from those he threatens. Any knowledgeable and intelligent astrologer armed with the birthdates of the world leaders and the planetary influences which govern their countries can map out the course of a future conflict years in advance.

What Icke has been guided to discover is the principle that predictions are made on the condition that everything continues on its present course. However, it only takes one enlightened person in a position of influence, such as the Indian nationalist leader and pacifist Mahatma Gandhi, acting contrary to expectation to defuse a confrontation and avert disaster.

Icke's 'mission', therefore, is to awaken us to our Higher Nature, our True Self, so that we will act in accordance with the Universal Laws and not out of self-interest. Only then will the higher powers which watch over us cease to send us the warnings of disasters which the psychics foresee.

Unfortunately, Icke's enthusiasm tends to give wings to his imagination - an affliction suffered by many genuine psychics and seers through the centuries. His philosophy is sound, but his predictions are frequently waylaid by flights of fantasy.

*Gandhi (right) is an example of the unpredictable altering the course of events.*

# RAMALA – SPIRITS OF THE NEW AGE

**Glastonbury, in England, has long been known as a spiritual centre for occult and esoteric groups drawn by the legends of King Arthur and the Holy Grail. But in the mid-1970s it gave birth to a new group who claimed to have made telepathic contact with highly evolved spiritual beings and to have 'channelled' their prophecies for the New Age.**

*The purpose of the Ramala teachings is to help humanity to prepare for the Golden Age that is to come.*

*The Ramala Group's private sanctuary at Chalice Hill House, Glastonbury.*

Channelled teachings are nothing new. The Old Testament prophets were also mediums, in the truest sense, for the Divine message, only they called it Divine Inspiration. The influence of spirit guides was also a feature of the prophecies of Madame Blavatsky, Alice Bailey, Aleister Crowley and other figureheads of the occult fraternity, though it is more likely that these hypersensitive individuals had contacted their own alter-egos, their subconscious selves, judging by the quality and accuracy of their prophecies. However, in the past twenty years there has been a significant increase in these channelled teachings, due we are told, to groups such as the one at Glastonbury downloading the energy which will initiate the New Age.

Accepting the possibility that humanity may be encouraged in its evolution by benign spiritual beings requires a considerable leap of faith for many Western minds, but one only has to compare the channelled teachings recently published in the USA, India and Australia to be struck by the similarity. If these telepathic teachings are part of a genuine new phenomena then the so-called New Age will require a worldwide awakening to a far greater reality.

The beings, which the Glastonbury group refer to as The Ramala Teachers, were desperate to warn humanity of the choice it will have to make when the New Age dawns at the turn of the century. 'This is our supreme moment of choice, either to recognize or to deny our spiritual birthright,' the group explained in the first of two remarkable books publicizing the prophecies. '[...] The purpose of the Ramala teachings is to help humanity to prepare for this great moment of transformation and transmutation so that we may be ready for the Golden Age that is to come.'

*The Ramala Group's twelve-sided meditation centre where the New Age predictions have been channelled.*

The Teachers explained that humanity is ill-prepared for the great planetary changes that will usher in the new age and that now, in the last years before the new millennium, we must build a new ark, an 'ark of consciousness', to escape the deluge of negative forces which threatens to impede our progress.

Over a decade ten different beings made contact with the group who were based at the Ramala Sanctuary at Chalice Hill House, renamed the Sanctuary of the Holy Grail. There the group would meditate, building up an energy field to attract their spiritual guides who would then speak through the leader in much the same way as an interpreter would translate for a foreign visitor.

Through their spirit visitors the group learned that the coming Aquarian age is destined to be 'the greatest cycle in Humanity's evolutionary path', more important even than the current Piscean Age, which witnessed 'the grounding of the Christ energy' and which is to come to a violent, though unspecified, end.

*The Ramala Group published the channelled teachings in a series of privately published books.*

The 'cosmic energy pattern' for the coming age is present, but humanity must be tuned in to it and ground it, 'in just the same way as the Nazarene grounded the Christ Energy 2000 years ago ...There are souls of great evolution incarnating on the earth at this time ...It is therefore imperative that an environment be created where these great souls can manifest their true wisdom and potential ...'

# THE LATE, GREAT PLANET EARTH

The most dramatic prophecies came during the question and answer sessions which followed each telepathic talk. During one of these the group were told that in the far distant future the earth as we know it will die. Whether the end will come about through a natural lingering decay, or in the flash of a nuclear apocalypse, the Ramala Teachers would not say. But they gave assurances that a new and better world would emerge: '... the Earth, like you, is imbued with spirit. It will, therefore, never die ... its physical form might change as it experiences periods of transformation and transmutation ... in the same way that you in your physical bodies die and are born again onto a higher plane of life so the Earth, on another level undergoes a similar experience.'

The Ramala Teachers explained that this will not be the first time that the earth will emerge from the trials of rebirth:

'... the Lord of this Earth, the Goddess, the Earth Mother whose form it is, is a great and evolved spiritual being ... Humanity is now tampering with that sacred being, Mother Nature, in order to achieve short-term gain without considering the long-term implications.'

The results of our relentless exploitation of the earth's resources will be that all humanity will suffer the effects of drought, pestilence and famine, but not on the orders of an angry, omnipotent God, 'rather as the flowering of the seeds which Humanity itself has sown'.

# SAI BABA AND MOTHER MEERA — AVATARS OF THE NEW AGE

**According to the Hindu tradition, aspects of Brahma, the Supreme Being, return periodically to earth in the bodies of enlightened human beings known as avatars. At the present moment there are said to be two major avatars on earth, Sai Baba - whose appearance was foretold in ancient Hindu manuscripts - and a young Indian woman, Mother Meera. Their presence is said to indicate that humanity has reached a moment of supreme crisis.**

*Sai Baba, whose 'Mission of Love' was foretold by the prophet Shuka 3000 years ago.*

5600 years ago the Hindu prophets foretold a time, roughly corresponding to the present century, when civilization would be dominated by materialism and machines. It would be a time when humanity would possess the means to destroy itself, but be too proud to seek Divine intervention at the critical moment.

However, unlike the Western tradition which states that on the Day of Judgement God will personally pronounce sentence on 'the quick and the dead', the sacred scriptures of the Hindus prophesy the appearance of an 'Avatar of Love', who will reveal himself at the moment of crisis so that humanity can make a choice between light and darkness. The avatar will manifest not once, but on three critical occasions through history, the second of which is predicted for the end of the twentieth century.

The first incarnation of this avatar is said to have been the prophet Sai Baba of Shirdi who died in 1918 at the close of the First World War. Before he died he named the Indian province in which he would reincarnate eight years later, and this is where Sathya Sai Baba was born.

It is claimed that as a child Sathya immersed himself in philosophical discussions with devotees who had known him in his previous incarnation and that he could perform minor miracles, which he continues to do to this day. But he did not assume the mantle of the prophet until the age of fourteen when he fell into a trance, during which he proclaimed himself the reincarnation of Sai Baba of Shirdi and afterwards took his name.

Baba's devotees, of whom there are said to be over 50 million worldwide, cite further proof of his divinity in the form of the palmleaf prophecies, manuscripts written in 3000 BC by the Indian sage Shuka who accurately

*Sai Baba of Shirdi - said to be the first incarnation of the 'Avatar of Love'.*

predicted Baba's birthdate to the very day – 23 November 1926 – and named the village in which he would be born, although it did not exist during the sage's lifetime. Baba has said that his mission is to initiate a new Golden Age for the coming millennium, to balance the forces of chaos which have dominated our century.

'I have come to restore a golden chapter in the story of humanity, wherein falsehood will fail, truth will triumph, and virtue will reign. Character will confer power then, not knowledge, or inventive skill, or wealth. Wisdom will be enthroned in the councils of nations.'

> 'I am God; you too are God. The only difference is that I know it and you do not.'

But Baba's own prophecies speak of this Golden Age being created by man, not God. 'Man is living at the dawn of a Golden Age and he himself will determine the timing of the transition by his own acts and thoughts ... The arrival of the Golden Age will be heralded by a new coming, as well as some upheavals, sufficient to uproot the evil that is so prevalent today...'

These 'upheavals' will come at the turn of the century, and will take the form of natural disasters of Biblical proportions and a deepening crisis of conscience. Man will lose faith in orthodox religion and turn inward for peace and guidance while Baba will calm the restless forces of nature. The changes to come will be difficult for those with materialistic values to accept, he says, but without change there can be no progress or evolution.

'... there are signs of a new awakening. That awakening is in its early stages, but it will gradually spread to every corner of the globe ... Today you cannot visualize such a state because there is chaos everywhere, fighting, scheming, hatred, evil; all the negative emotions are in the ascendant. But eventually the change will come ... I assure you that very soon the dark clouds will be scattered and you will witness a happy era all over the world. Right will be restored and evil put down ...'

Most Westerners would not accept that one person could be the incarnation of an aspect of the Divine, or that he or she might be a more fully realized being from a higher spiritual plane. For the followers of Sai Baba and Mother Meera (see box), of which there are hundreds of thousands in the West, acceptance of such a concept marks the first step in their own spiritual evolution. As Baba has said, 'I am God; you too are God. The only difference is that I know it and you do not.'

## THE DIVINE MOTHER

Mother Meera, a young Indian woman currently living in the tiny village of Dornburg-Thalheim, Germany, is believed to be the latest incarnation of Kali the Divine Mother. Each year her presence attracts thousands of spiritual seekers from all over the world who consider her the avatar of the New Age.

'The possibility for mankind to evolve and change is always there whether or not an Avatar comes,' she explains. 'People naturally believe in a greater reality. However, when an Avatar comes people feel the possibility more and aspire more strongly ... The consciousness of mankind is being prepared for great leaps and discoveries - in a gentle way wherever possible ... God is giving man a great chance ... Now man must choose.'

The violence of this century, she says, was necessary to awaken humanity to the consequences of being self-centred, of living without God-consciousness. Once we accept this, the next stage in our spiritual evolution will begin.

'This leap is certain. It will happen. It is happening now ... There is no time to waste ...'

The New Age will come when we accept that the crisis we face is of our own making and not that of an exterior force created by us as a convenient scapegoat for our own failings.

*Kali, the Mother Goddess, embodies the feminine aspect of the Divine.*

# THE CELESTINE PROPHECY

**The predictions and positive philosophy outlined in** *The Celestine Prophecy*, **James Redfield's million-selling spiritual adventure story, makes the perfect antidote to the apocalyptic visions of the past. Its nine key insights into the secrets of life have awoken a new generation to the possible destiny of mankind and ensured its author the status of a New Age guru.**

*James Redfield's prophetic insights have ensured him instant elevation to the role of New Age guru.*

Since its publication in 1994 *The Celestine Prophecy* has been adopted as a guidebook for the New Age. Its author James Redfield, an American sociologist and counsellor, compiled his philosophy from the ancient wisdom traditions of East and West, but he has presented these truths in a unique and inspired form – that of an adventure parable peppered with interlinking spiritual secrets and predictions for the coming new millennium.

The context is essentially fictional, but the insights revealed constitute the stuff of esoteric teachings from the early Jewish mystics to the New Age movements of our own time.

The author details a series of apparently coincidental meetings with various strangers who have each been privileged to see a part of an ancient Peruvian manuscript written in Aramaic. None of them has managed to study the entire manuscript because of the Church's efforts to suppress it, therefore each imparts a different insight into the course of human spiritual evolution as revealed by the manuscript, but only when the author has reached the stage of development where he is ready to ask the appropriate question.

The First Insight is that everything that happens in our lives has a purpose and is part of a universal plan. What we perceive as coincidences are designed to awaken us to the inherent mystery of life and lead us to our true destiny. We have the free will to recognize and follow these signs, or to ignore them.

The Second Insight declares that at the end of the second millennium, as we approach the year 2000, we will acquire a fresh perception of the past thousand years and in so doing will clearly identify the dominant theme of the Modern Age, giving us a guide into the next millennium.

The Third Insight predicts that we will be vitalized by a new force which will heighten our perception of

> The insights revealed constitute the stuff of esoteric teachings from the early Jewish mystics to the New Age movements of our own time.

the subtle energies that pervade the universe, sharpening our psychic senses.

The Fourth Insight follows on from the third in foreseeing that having heightened our awareness of the universe, we will be more acutely aware of our alienation from the source of creation. Instead of seeking the source and drawing on its energy through spiritual disciplines, such as meditation, most of the human race have been compensating by draining the life energy from other human beings through vain attempts to control and dominate them.

The Fifth Insight is the realization that the universal life force can provide all the energy we need, if only we will open ourselves to it.

The Sixth Insight reveals that our habit of using and manipulating other people stems from the techniques we used to secure attention when we were children. The destiny of humanity is to find a higher meaning of life and kick this habit.

The Seventh Insight says that we can only mature as spiritual beings when we lose our dependence on other people and discover our true selves. Once we have done this we will

The Celestine Prophecy *describes how our destinies are linked with that of the Universe.*

discover why we were born into a particular family and what lessons we are to learn in life. What has been called the New Age generation are now becoming conscious of this truth and once they have grasped it the process will accelerate.

The penultimate insight states that we are each, individually, inextricably bound up in the evolution of the entire species.

The Ninth Insight details the changes in human consciousness in the next millennium (see box).

The incredible popularity of *The Celestine Prophecy* and other similar New Age publications proves that there is a substantial demand for positive, self-help guides at this critical moment in human evolution. They are an antidote to the perverse philosophies and predictions of the apocalyptic prophets of the sinister cults who are exploiting the fears of their followers.

## PARADISE ON EARTH

The final prediction of *The Celestine Prophecy* describes the world as it will be in the next millennium, after humanity has been inspired by the revelation of the nine insights to create a paradise on earth. It predicts that we will choose to control population growth so that each of us will have more space to live in and it envisages the establishment of an increasing number of idyllic places as alternative living centres. The forests will be allowed to grow unhindered so that their trees can become a source of spiritual energy. By the year 2500 AD much of mankind will be living in this new Garden of Eden, but within easy access of urban areas offering the latest technological advances.

By that time human evolution will have progressed to a point where we will no longer feel the need to control others or amass possessions to gain a sense of security. Consumerism will be a thing of our primitive past. We will instead be living in what will be called a 'spiritual economy' in which no one will prosper at the expense of another. A reliance on science and the work ethic will have been replaced by a universal pursuit of the Truth.

*Redfield predicts a return to Eden if we rediscover our spiritual selves.*

# CONCLUSION

A lthough our fascination with the future has its origins in the basic instinct for survival, our preoccupation with prophecies and predictions stems from what the mystics would call a 'divine discontent' with the world as it is. We may sometimes affect the attitudes of a fatalist or pessimist for the outside world, but inwardly most of us harbour an innate desire to make the world a better place.

It is this inner vision which has driven the innovators, inventors, scientists, philosophers and social reformers to drag humanity from the Dark Ages to the Space Age in the relatively short time of a single millennium. It is this inner vision which has shaped both the past and the present and which will surely determine our future more substantially than the pronouncements of the prophets – no matter how well-intentioned these may be.

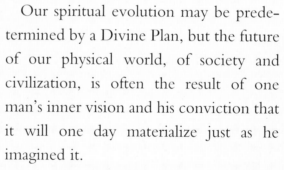

Our spiritual evolution may be predetermined by a Divine Plan, but the future of our physical world, of society and civilization, is often the result of one man's inner vision and his conviction that it will one day materialize just as he imagined it.

Of course, it could be argued that those prophets who were genuine channels of Divine Inspiration have not been as influential as they might have been because either they were not able to forcefully convey the real meaning of their message – language being limited to the expression of human, and not Divine, experience –, or

that due to our own limited capacity for understanding we have not been able to grasp the true meaning of what they tried to convey.

Whichever is true, the Piscean Age, which astrologers would claim has determined the course of human history for the past 2,000 years, has been characterized by a vain attempt to formularize and institutionalize spirituality through the format of orthodox religion. We are promised that the coming Age of Aquarius, whose exact date is still hotly debated by astrologers, will harness the energies of trans-formation, so that the new millennium will offer the promise of enlightenment for all who embrace it. But we must have the will as well as the vision to bring this about.

No longer can we ignore the debilitating influence on our progress and spiritual evolution exerted by those who, through ignorance or design, have corrupted the revelations of the true teachers and prophets. These superfluous, self-appointed intermediaries between man and the Divine – be they cult leaders, despotic religious officials, or esoteric eccentrics – embody the other side of our nature, the apparently equal urge for self-deprecation and self-destruction which has seen humanity take one step backwards for every two paces it has taken forwards. But progress we will over the next millennium, and the next, *ad infinitum*, until the inexorable momentum of evolution perfects the human spirit to the point where it can rejoin its source, which will have been strengthened by the process.

The true purpose of prophecy is revelation, but its underlying theme is that of the eternal struggle between Good and Evil, the two aspects of our own personalities _ the light of wisdom against the darkness of

ignorance. This perennial battle, embodied in the Biblical image of Armageddon, continues to hold a fearful fascination for those brought up in the Judaeo-Christian culture. But all cultures, races and religions which look for salvation outside the individual share this obsession.

When we do not accept the need to resolve this conflict within ourselves, as some of the Eastern religions, or philosophies, encourage its members to do, then we project it onto external forces in the

form of archetypes, such as angels and demons or, as is all too often the case, against those we consider our enemies. We all have the tendency to assume the role of the righteous and project our more unpleasant characteristics onto others, just as nations have done throughout history when justifying the persecution of their neighbours or ethnic minorities. However, this reconciling of our Higher Self and our primitive, Shadow Self, is the real battle of Armageddon, and it is that we must resolve if we are to eventually bring into being the